MAKING FAMILY LAW

The legislative process is complex, encompassing a variety of aims and outcomes. Some norms and rules are embodied in law because we are simply expected by government to follow them. Others are there for entirely different reasons. A legislator may wish to send messages about what constitutes desirable behaviour, to demonstrate government's ability to deal with a local and short-term issue or to distract the electorate from other crises. Law is often, though not always, designed as a means to an end. Taking a sociological and empirically-based approach, this book offers a rare insight into the real processes by which lawmakers attempt to influence (or fail to influence) human behaviour.

This account of the legislative process in Westminster rests on the author's observations and discussion with key players from the standpoint of an academic adviser on research to the department responsible for family law-making (originally the Lord Chancellor's department, then the Department for Constitutional Affairs and now the Ministry of Justice) and draws on her longstanding involvement in and knowledge of the processes of law-making. Documenting the little understood processes that occur in Whitehall, in particular how ministers, advisers and officials work together, it reveals a quite different picture from that of the rational lawmaker imagined in textbooks. Instead what emerges is an empirically-based view of the aims and functions of statute law including the different forms and relevance of symbolic legislation and a realistic view of what law aims to accomplish and what can be done in practice.

Making Family Law

A Socio-Legal Account of Legislative Process in England and Wales, 1985–2010

Mavis Maclean
with Jacek Kurczewski

•HART•
PUBLISHING
OXFORD AND PORTLAND, OREGON
2011

Published in the United Kingdom by Hart Publishing Ltd
16C Worcester Place, Oxford, OX1 2JW
Tel: +44 (0)1865 517530
Fax: +44 (0)1865 510710
Email: mail@hartpub.co.uk
Website: www.hartpub.co.uk

Published in North America (US and Canada) by
Hart Publishing
c/o International Specialized Book Services
920 NE 58th Avenue, Suite 300
Portland, OR 97213-3786
USA
Tel: +1 (503) 287-3093 or toll-free: 1 (800) 944-6190
Fax: +1 (503) 280-8832
Email: orders@isbs.com
Website: www.isbs.com

British Library Cataloguing in Publication Data
Data Available

ISBN: 978-1-84946-227-3

Typeset by Hope Services, Abingdon
Printed and bound in Great Britain by
Lightning Source UK Ltd

Acknowledgements

We wish to thank the Rockefeller Foundation for giving us a joint residency at the Bellagio Centre in Bellagio, Italy. We were able to take the time to talk, draft and redraft in the company of fellow scholarly residents in surroundings of great beauty but also intellectual stimulation. We particularly thank Monroe Price and Janine Wedel for their support and Peter Harris for sharing his knowledge so generously.

Contents

Preface

The legislative process is complex, encompassing a variety of aims and outcomes. Some norms and rules are embodied in law because we are simply expected by government to follow them. Others are there for entirely different reasons. A legislator may wish to send messages about what constitutes desirable behaviour, to demonstrate government's ability to deal with a local and short-term issue or to distract the electorate from other crises. Law is often, though not always, designed as a means to an end.

This study of the making of family law in England and Wales draws on the longstanding relationship between the law faculties in Oxford and Warsaw and will be accompanied by a companion volume, which will look at law-making in post-communist Poland.[1] Both studies take a sociological and empirically based perspective. When the empirical study of law began at the end of the nineteenth century and legal thinkers began to introduce this approach into jurisprudence, Leon Petrażycki's, a Russian scholar of Polish origin, pointed to the role of interests and power in social relations. He suggested that jurisprudence, with its focus on rules – whether written, oral or behavioural – fails to take into account the real processes through which law influences (or fails to influence) human behaviour. In order to have influence the law must have a direct impact on individuals, through what Petrażycki described as a psychological processes involving 'legal emotions'.[2] In his view, we act in a certain way because we think we are obliged to an entity, which may be known as God, as the State or simply as the Law. The law exists through our readiness to do something we feel we are obliged to do, or as our right to do something which others will be obliged to accept. The ideas of individuals about how they will act often differ from what is assumed by lawyers and authorities to be the law, but the skill of lawmakers is to either bring human motivation closer to the legislative project or bring

[1] *Law-Making: Politics, Process and Practice; an Empirical Study of Legislative Process in Poland, 1989–2006* (with Jacek Kurczewski) (forthcoming).

[2] L Petrażycki, *Law and Morality*, HW Babb (trans) (Harvard University Press Cambridge, MA, 1995).

the project closer to what could be achieved given a particular state of legal emotion, bearing in mind that there are various motivations for compliance with the law, including simply habit.A scientific or rational legal policy, according to Petrazycki, would consist of law-making based on sound and systematic knowledge of the processes that lead towards the outcome desired by the legislator.

Petrazycki was regarded by contemporaries was as naïvely psychological in his theory of law, but his approach fits the empirical sociology of law developed in the twentieth century so well that he has now been accepted as one of its founders. In 1913 he formulated his central idea in these words:

> The essence of legal policy issues lies in the scientifically grounded explanation of the consequences that one should expect on introducing legal regulation and in the development of such principles that, if introduced through legislation, would bring about a particular and predictable result. The tasks of a legal policy maker are therefore: firstly to manage individual and group conduct through legal motivation; and secondly to improve the human psyche through reducing malicious, antisocial tendencies and implanting and strengthening the opposite.[3]

The first of these tasks is addressed by lawmakers at all times and in all places. As to the second, debate about human progress continues.

[3] Ibid, 156–57.

1

Introduction

THIS ACCOUNT OF the legislative process in Westminster rests on the author's observations and discussion with key players in her role as an academic adviser on research to the department responsible for family law-making, known in 1985 as the Lord Chancellor's Department, then as the Department for Constitutional Affairs and, by the time of writing, as the Ministry of Justice. Any such personal account is only that, and this claims to be no more. It risks getting things horribly wrong. But having read and reread the existing literature, in particular Michael Zander's account *The Law-Making Process*, first published in 1980 and in its most recent edition in 2004, it seemed that there might be value in giving an account of the hitherto little documented stages of the process that occurs in Whitehall, in particular how ministers and officials work together. Zander stated early on in his first edition that 'very little has been written about the process of preparing legislation from Whitehall's perspective',[1] citing only a conference paper given in the mid-1970s on penal policy by Michael Moriarty.[2]

Traditional models of the law-making process tend to assume the rationality of the lawmakers.[3] There is a presumption that a domain can be systematically described, and a law can be devised that is complete and unambiguous in its expression. If law-making is indeed a rational intellectual activity, and the law itself is instrumentally rational, then a precise goal could be defined, and the provisions of that law, if followed in practice, would lead to the fulfilment of that goal. In critical legal studies, on the other hand, it is argued that the process is almost the

[1] M Zander, *The Law-Making Process*, 1st edn (London, Weidenfeld and Nicholson, 1980).

[2] M Moriarty, 'The Policy-Making Process: How It Is Seen from the Home Office' in N Walker (ed), *Penal Policy-Making* in England (Cambridge, Institute of Criminology, 1977) 132–9. The paper describes Ministers as not often bringing in fresh policy ideas but working creatively and with political drive upon ideas, proposals, reports, etc that are, so to speak, already to hand within the department or in the surrounding world of academic penal thinking.

[3] For example, see L Petrażycki, *Law and Morality*, HW Babb (trans) (Cambridge, MA, Harvard University Press, 1995).

reverse. In this formulation, the law-making process is similarly held to be directed by idealised presumptions, but these are held to be based not on reason but on the interests of individual lawmakers.[4]

While accepting the value of both these approaches, this book is written from the perspective of the sociology of law. We draw on personal observation and interview to focus on the social nature of the legislative process, and by commenting on the social process and interaction involved we try to penetrate what Francis Snyder has called the opaque nature of the law-making process. We offer an empirically grounded study of the making of statute law in England and Wales for family matters over the last twenty years. We make reference to the law-making processes in other jurisdictions to highlight the special features of the Westminster process as revealed by comparison. In particular, we have drawn on the historic connection between the law faculties in Oxford and Warsaw, as well as the presence of Adam Podgorecki as Co-Director of the Oxford Centre for Socio-Legal Studies, which led to a close relationship with the Institute for the Study of Custom and Law in Warsaw, headed for many years by Jacek Kurczewski. Over the period 1985 to 2010 the work of rebuilding Polish democracy required the legislative process to become visible and explicit, as alternative processes were discussed and decisions made. Our lengthy discussions over the years of these developments have often cast fresh light on our understanding of parallel processes in London. This collaboration, together with our debt to Michael Zander for providing the first detailed description of the law-making in the Law and Society Series,[5] will we hope permit us to add some insights to the details drawn from empirical observation.

What is Law-making?

Following in the traditions of Leon Petrażycki (1867–1931), the founder of the social science approach to the politics of law, we accept the role of law in reinforcing rather than creating new ways of thinking and acting. And following the development by Adam Podgorecki (1925–98) of this view during his term as Joint Director of the Oxford Centre for Socio-

[4] F Snyder, 'Thinking about Interests: Legislative Process in the European Community' in J Starr and J Collier (eds), *History and Power in the Study of Law* (Ithaca, Cornell University Press, 1989) 168–201.

[5] Zander (above n 1).

Legal Studies, we accept too the need to study both the expected and unexpected outcomes of any piece of legislation. Law-making in the Petrażycki/Podgorecki formulation is understood as a purposeful, instrumental and reflexive rational activity, requiring self-reflection by the lawmaker, who uses scientific rational methods to monitor continually the possible and actual effects of a piece of law.[6] But in the light of our experience, we take a rather different approach, which is a little less optimistic about the role of reason.

Drawing on our observations and experiences we suggest that there is another set of analyses to be made of the interpersonal network of roles and relationships that constitute the law-making process as a complex social activity, the goals of which are sometimes almost forgotten, often unclear and always negotiated between the participants involved in the project. There are deals to be done. As Ronald Dworkin has said in his commentary on legislative intention, if we look for evidence about the state of mind of those who prepare a statue so that we may interpret it correctly, whose thoughts should be examined?[7] Should the thoughts of every member of the Congress that enacted it be considered, including those who voted against it? Are the thoughts of those who spoke most often more important than the thoughts of others? And 'what about the executive officials and assistants who prepared the initial drafts? What about the head of state who signed the act and made it law? What about the private citizens who wrote letters to their representatives, what about the lobbies and action groups?'[8] Any realistic view of the legislative process must include the impact of all these actors.

Who Makes Law?

In this account of how legislation is created at Westminster, we begin with the assumption that in Britain, an established democracy, there is a clear division between the role of elected politicians and those of public servants and stakeholders. The importance of this division can be seen more clearly by making reference to Poland, a re-established democracy,

[6] See K Motyka, 'Leon Petracycki: Challenge to Legal Orthodoxy', 23rd IVR World Congress (Krakow, 1–6 Aug 2007).

[7] R Dworkin, *Law's Empire* (Cambridge, MA, Belknap Press of Harvard University Press, 1986).

[8] Ibid, 313.

where the ambiguity of these distinctions has remained during the process of changing from state regulation to democratic legislation.

We have been fortunate in being able to draw on not only our experience as academic sociologists of law but also our direct experience of law-making. Maclean has studied legal policy-making, especially in family law, as an academic in Oxford and has also observed the law-making process from within government sitting in Whitehall as the Academic Adviser to the Lord Chancellor's Department (later the Department for Constitutional Affairs and now the Ministry of Justice) since 1997. Kurczewski has studied the sociology of custom and law in Poland and many other settings. He also took part in the Round Table Discussions that were a key part of the transformation process in Poland in 1989 and became the Deputy Vice Marshall of the first elected assembly of the Sejm in 1992.These experiences are recorded in his book *Living Sociology of Law* published in 2010[9] We have looked behind the scenes in the Houses of Parliament and the Polish Sejm, taken part in the informal social gatherings where ideas are formulated, support is gathered and alliances are negotiated. We have participated in ministerial meetings and committees; observed the relationship between the politicians seeking to initiate change and the officials and draftsmen who are given responsibility for putting these ideas into practice; and seen the attempts of external interested stakeholders to influence the process. Any sociologically based account of the process of law has to include a description of these relationships between the individuals who work together, not always willingly, on particular projects that begin as broad political ideas but must then be refined and nuanced until they are politically acceptable to the electorate, clear enough to make drafting possible and capable of being implemented. In describing and analysing this process we draw a distinction between lawmakers who 'own' and drive forward the law to be made on the one hand and law-workers who actually engage in its production on the other hand.

The Purpose and Limitations of Law-making

The case studies presented here come from our own experience, but we hope to take this socio-legal reflection on the law-making process beyond a merely anecdotal collection of examples towards developing an empirically based view of the aims and functions of statute law. For governments

[9] J Kurczewski, *Living Sociology of Law* (Warsaw, University of Warsaw Press, 2010).

with an acute awareness of the power of the media and the need to maintain their majorities in forthcoming elections, it is all too easy to turn to symbolic legislation as a tool to communicate messages about high-profile issues, and this practice is easy to criticise. We look therefore at the different forms of symbolic law-making and what it can achieve. We also look at the limits of law-making, exploring the boundaries of what is possible.

It is important to distinguish between what law aims to accomplish and what can be done in practice. To take an example from English family law, legal regulation cannot stop individuals harming their partners or children. But it can give clear signals that this behaviour is unacceptable and punishable. The law cannot create the resources needed to support a family that has separated into more than one household, but it can insist that the existing resources are fairly distributed. Nonetheless, there are always policy goals that can never be attained through legislation. For example, a recent report endorsed by the Conservative Party and entitled 'Every Family Matters' seeks to use the law to promote marriage, in order to mend what the authors call 'Broken Britain' and to move away from what is described as a culture of family breakdown.[10] This report attributes blame for high divorce rates in part to the law and ancillary procedures, which are said to be causally implicated in high rates of family breakdown. But to those who have studied the working of family law, it seems improbable that any legislative change will substantially affect the ways in which men and women organise their private lives. Any attempt to reform the law in order to make people good and happy is unrealistic.

The Legislative Context

The need to facilitate a more realistic approach from legislators, together with a reformulation of public expectations, is a key driver for our work. The cases presented herein arose under different political and organisational contexts. Some involved governments with large majorities, which facilitate purposive legislative activity, while others involved governments constrained by the struggle to maintain their hold on power. There were times when teams of experienced and skilful public servants with carefully defined roles were able to work together throughout a legislative project, and times when external consultants played a strong

[10] Family Law Review, 'Every Family Matters: An In-Depth Review of Family Law in Britain' (Centre for Social Justice, 2009).

part or when individual activists were highly visible. The press is always a factor in determining government action in a democracy, but there were occasions when press involvement was particularly visible, when the media took a clear position and pressed hard for a particular course of action, exerting influence on ministers.

We look at the role of the Parliamentary processes for scrutiny and review in giving rise to pressure for reform. We will also point to cases that highlight the idiosyncratic nature of law-making as a collective social enterprise. Even in those rare cases in which a legislative initiative can be attributed to a single individual, any legal proposal that is highly personalised must still become acceptable to a number of collective bodies both in government and outside in order to obtain legitimacy and be capable of being implemented. As part of the normal process of group activity, the development of mutual understanding or, if this is impossible, the acceptance of the need to present a unified front is important in order to make progress, as law-making is a sequential process with many stages.

Development of Legislative Content

As part of this sequential process, we observed the unfolding of various levels of meaning during the work of preparing specific laws. Each form of words opened up the possibility of competing interpretations, which needed to be reconciled, at least in part. But each on-going working interpretation is also reflexive and leads to wider formulations that are not necessarily part of the original purpose of the law; alternatively, a part of the original design may be excluded.

The practical process of law-making is made more difficult for law-workers by the lack of continuity in the underlying assumptions. Changes in the expectations about what is wanted from the law are constantly brought about by political pressures from outside the process, as well as by the law-workers involved in the process themselves. These sources of change include ministers, who guide particular matters through the legislative assembly; officials, who work with them to facilitate this process; and legal draftsmen, who provide the text and advise on relevant precedents.

Anglo–Polish Comparisons

As we have mentioned above, the origins of this book lie in the wish of the two authors to share their conversations about the experience of legislative process over the past twenty years. In the late 1980s when transformation from authoritarian communist rule began in Poland there was a perception that many of the problems experienced could not occur in the free West. It was a surprise to both of us to find that some of the restrictions felt in Central Europe were in fact familiar to those living under the longstanding Conservative government led by Prime Minster Thatcher, and that Britons might learn from the experience of colleagues in Central and Eastern Europe how to develop ways of getting around some of the bureaucratic and legalistic hurdles we all were facing.

For example, in Oxford, publication of a small study of judicial decision-making in divorce cases was delayed by the then Lord Chancellor, Lord Hailsham, as the study caused government embarrassment by revealing the degree of variation in the exercise of the matrimonial jurisdiction of registrars.[11] In Warsaw in 1980, on the other hand, a parallel study of decision-making by the judiciary in family courts could be published as soon as it was completed, though in small numbers with frequent new editions, as censorship did not apply to print runs of less than one hundred copies.[12] An elected government in England with a long period in power and a comfortable majority could thus behave in a quite authoritarian manner. In Poland, on the other hand, the traditions of democracy and freedom of expression died hard: the rules of censorship could be accommodated. In England, freedom of expression, though taken for granted, is not always easily achieved. These 'Alice through the Looking Glass' experiences have helped us to think harder about the origins and outcomes of the law-making process.

Stages in the Legislative Process

Under Adam Podgorecki's formulation for legal reform,[13] at the design stage a problem will have been identified on which there is wide agreement that something must be done but often little agreement as to what action is desirable, never mind feasible. A policy will then be proposed, and a programme of action must be prepared. This involves firstly a procedural plan, then the anticipation of likely problems, followed by redesign until all serious reservations have been overcome. The final stage in

[11] B Barrington Baker, C Clarke, S Raikes and J Eekelaar, 'The Matrimonial Jurisdiction of Registrars' (Oxford Centre for Socio-Legal Studies, 1977).

[12] M Fuszara, 'The Judges Room', mimeo (1980), later published in M Fuszara, *Family, Gender and Body* (Warsaw, The University of Warsaw, 1990).

[13] A Podgorecki, 'Three Levels of Functioning of Law' in A Podgorecki, J Alexander and R Shields (eds), *Social Engineering* (Ottawa, Carleton University Press, 1996).

Podgorecki's typology is 'action', when a policy or project must be piloted and tested. This 'road testing' not only helps to identify further problems but also can help to create a culture of compliance among the key stakeholders, which will facilitate implementation. And finally the process and outcome of a new project must be evaluated.

This structure offers a useful framework. But in addition to this linear process, we will be looking also at the interactions and relationships between those involved in the law-making process, as well as the impact these may have on the direction of change. Different skills come into play at the various stages, and part of our story is about the stresses that occur when responsibility passes from one set of law-workers to another at every level, minister to official, official to draftsman, draftsmen to legislative assembly and back through the stages of amendment to the political owners of the policy. Not only different skills but also different strengths are displayed by the various players. A government minister has the power to demand action or to veto a project; but without the substantive knowledge and the technical skills of his or her staff the minister can do little. Similarly, the legislative assembly has the power to accept, reject or amend proposed legislation; but in a parliamentary system in which party discipline is firmly maintained, this power, too, depends on decisions made by party leaders in government. The lawyer who drafts the actual words of a bill has no power to do other than take instruction from his or her political masters, but at the end of the day this detailed work also plays a large part in determining the form of the resulting legislation. In the case of the Children Act (England and Wales) 1989, for example, it was the skill of the draftsman that finally enabled the Bill to go before Parliament. For when the managers of Parliamentary time insisted that the number of clauses to be discussed must be strictly limited, to an extent that would have made the Bill unworkable, the draftsman redefined the sections of the Bill as schedules rather than clauses, and the Bill was presented and passed.

British Legislative Procedure

In England and Wales statute law is the most visible part of the regulatory framework, but it is only one part of the law-making system; it is supported by the decisions of the judiciary, who provide binding precedents, and augmented by layers of regulations, which can be made by Parliament without any vote being taken. This study is limited to statutory reform.

Although Parliament is the legislative body in name, in practice it is government that makes the law in the sense of choosing from the multiplicity of ideas for legislative reform and seeking, though not necessarily following, the advice of public officials or civil servants, who are asked by ministers to look into the feasibility and desirability of any proposal. When a policy issue has been identified as requiring a legislative response, the Minister for the relevant department must seek policy approval and drafting authority from Cabinet colleagues. The stimulus for action will range from considered responses to lengthy governmental inquiries into major spending issues, such as the structure of the pensions system, to rapid symbolic responses to specific items of immediate public concern. A famous English example of the latter is the Dangerous Dogs Act 1991, which was hurried through to permit the destruction or muzzling of certain breeds of dog after an incident in which a small child was mauled to death. But the legislation was unclear and unenforceable, and instead of arousing public support, it led instead to a reaction against the government from a nation well known to be animal lovers.

Policy officials working to a Minister will need his or her input and approval throughout the process. They will work in consultation with key stakeholders such as the judiciary, the legal profession and pressure groups. If the matter crosses the responsibilities of more than one government department there may be interdepartmental meetings or the setting up of working groups. It is a lengthy and complex process to reach the point at which the policy requirements are clearly enough expressed to be passed to the departmental solicitor, who will give instructions to Parliamentary counsel to start drafting a bill. Ministers vary from highly experienced and knowledgeable about their areas to new appointees to government, on steep and highly visible learning curves. There were anecdotes circulating after the Labour Government took office in 1997 after ten years in opposition that business in Whitehall came to halt for some days in some departments as the new Ministers did not realise that the Red Boxes containing papers sent to them for their attention by their officials required responses. Responses could be either 'yes', 'no' or 'no decision as yet', but until the papers were returned with some form of acknowledgment the officials could take no further action.

Ministers also vary in their social and managerial skills, ranging from charming and efficient to neither of the above. Some get on well with ministerial colleagues and work well in the Parliamentary setting. Others do not. Some work well with senior civil servants, asking good questions and listening to answers. Others do not. Similarly, some senior officials can help a Minister apparently effortlessly to achieve his or her aims. Others find it more difficult. Some are more effective than others in matching ministerial aims to feasible and desirable policy outcomes. The British television series *Yes Minister*, which featured a Permanent Secretary who manipulated not only his own minister but also on occasion the entire cabinet, was written by someone who knew Whitehall well.

The British system draws clear lines between the responsibilities of officials and the work of Ministers. There are safeguards to promote transparency and accountability in the requirement to take a note of every meeting held and to secure the agreement of those present to the note, including the record of action to be taken. But there is considerable room for manipulation by minute-takers and some laxity over recording informal conversations during a meeting's coffee break. (A standard ploy when seeking an un-minuted conversation is to invite the intended respondent over to a side-table, saying 'Can I get you a coffee . . .') Good use can also be made of chance meetings in the elevator. Those at the Department of Constitutional Affairs at one time had a propensity to break down, providing ample scope for in-depth private conversation. The email system is a record of everyday activity, and electronic record-keeping makes recorded information available to everyone in the department. However, email can be used defensively, for example, to say after a difficult meeting, 'Following our conversation, I would just like to confirm . . .' then to give the writer's chosen and possibly nuanced version of the event. The Freedom of Information Act 2000 makes any such item available to a member of the public on request (with exceptions for matters of security), but as the person requesting the item has to ask for the message by its title, another tactic to secure privacy is to send email messages with bizarrely inaccurate titles that would make it impossible for another person to identify the message.

When a Bill is in preparation, the Minister must gain collective agreement from ministerial colleagues that it will form part of the legislative programme, and unless it is minor and uncontroversial it will be announced in the government's programme by the Queen in her speech at the opening of Parliament, traditionally in November. There are tense days before the announcement of what will be included, as Ministers argue behind the scenes for the merits of their particular initiatives. Those likely to be popular with the Prime Minister's office tend to include those that will be popular with press and public but will not give rise to increased public spending. As part of the legislative programme, a Bill will next be introduced in one of the Houses of Parliament and be given a formal first reading. The next stage is a second reading, which usually triggers debate on the merits of the Bill. The committee stage follows, in which a Standing Committee of MPs will examine the legislation in great detail. The report stage follows, in which the Bill, with any amendments that have been accepted, is reported back to the whole House and again debated and possibly amended further. Given a governmental majority in the House of Commons, if an amendment that government cannot accept is brought to a vote, the government is unlikely to be defeated. In the House of Lords a Labour government tends to run a higher risk of defeat as there is still a large group of hereditary peers who accept the instructions of the Conservative whips, the members who organise voting behaviour on party lines.But any decision unacceptable to the Lords cannot be blocked for long under the Parliament Acts of 1911 and 1914, against the wishes of the Commons, known euphemistically as 'another place'. Procedure and progress under the Coalition government that formed in 2010 remain to be seen. Finally, there is the third Reading, following which the Bill is approved for sending up to the Lords if it originated in the Commons, or to the Commons if it originated in the Lords. The whole process is then repeated in the other House. If the Bill has not been amended, it passes to the Monarch for Royal Assent, whereupon it becomes law. If it has been amended, it goes back and forth between the two Houses until they agree on a text, which then goes forward for Royal Assent. The date for an Act which has completed every stage to be commenced may be set out in the statute or may be left open.

We have recently experienced the development of more systematic pre-legislative and post-legislative scrutiny. If a government Bill is published in advance as a Command Paper it need no longer be referred to the relevant departmental Select Committee of MPs, but instead a temporary committee (such as a Joint Committee of both the Commons and the Lords) can be appointed to consider it. There is no requirement for this to happen, and the Bills to be put forward in draft form for scrutiny are selected by the government's business managers. But increasing use is being made of the process, even though it takes departmental resources and can add to the length of time a Bill takes to reach the statute book. Such a committee can take oral and written evidence and suggest amendments, which a Minister may be more relaxed about accepting than amendments coming at a later stage when the Bill is in Parliament, where defeat would be more visible. The committee can look at Human Rights implications (though the Joint Committee on Human Rights looks at all draft Bills to assess their compliance with the European Convention on Human Rights and other internationally accepted human rights standards), at spending implications, at regulatory impact assessments and at delegated powers. It is generally agreed that this scrutiny has ensured more serious public debate of draft legislation than under the previous system and a more consensual, better-informed process without a vote being taken. The members of such a committee have the time to become well informed and can make more expert contributions to debate when the Bill is formally introduced into Parliament, whether in committee or debate. The Constitutional Affairs Committee of MPs took the view that draft bills are appropriate where there is any significant proposal which is complex, introduces fundamental change, and is controversial.[14] The Modernisation Committee's report of 1997 saw this work as helping to connect members of the public as individuals and as organised groups with the legislative process by making discussion more informal and accessible.

There has been slower progress, however, at the other end of the process, in other words, with post-legislative scrutiny. This is the process by which Parliament might review and evaluate the effects and consequences of an Act following its implementation. Parliament currently tends to regard its work as complete when a Bill is enacted. But in 2004 the Lords Constitution Committee gave the post-legislative scrutiny process strong support:

> Legislation may not fulfil its intended purpose. That may come to the Parliament's attention if there are palpable negative consequences. It may not come to Parliament's attention at all if it simply has no effect . . . [R]egular scrutiny will determine if Acts have done what they were intended to achieve; if not, it may then be possible to identify alternative means of achieving those goals. Scrutiny may also have the effect of ensuring that those who are meant to be implementing the measure are in fact implementing them in the way intended.[15]

There is, however, concern that the addition of any further functions to the workload of Parliament is counterproductive, given the pressure on Parliamentary time and resources. It is argued that a number of Bills now already include a requirement for the relevant department to monitor the impact of legislation (eg, the Anti-Social Behaviour Bill required the Home Office to monitor the effect of Anti-Social Behaviour Orders); and all regulatory impact assessments are routinely monitored. Nonetheless, in the view of the Hansard Society, given that law-making is a central function of Parliament, and one that attracts considerable criticism, the establishment of post-legislative scrutiny could deter poor drafting; require Parliament to consider the implications of legislation; and provide a mechanism for those outside who have been affected by legislation to feed their views into

[14] Hansard Society, 'Issues in Law-Making 6: Post-Legislative Scrutiny' Briefing paper (May 2005).

[15] Ibid.

the process.[16] Such a process might have an impact on the current practice of setting far distant implementation dates for legislation that requires the setting up of new agencies or services, in the hope that long delay will make the project out of date. When statutory obligations such as these are costly or controversial, delay tactics allow a government to engage in what may be termed symbolic legislation.

Taking a Bill through Parliament is a major and high-profile task that is always entrusted to a separate team of officials. There is a considerable workload for officials, especially at the Committee stage. This includes liaising between advisers and stakeholders; spotting where difficult questions are coming from; seeking to reassure anxious interested parties; preparing briefing for the government in response to proposed amendments; providing 'lines to take' to the departmental press office in response to media interest; and at all times supporting the Minister. But for officials, there will always be another Bill in the future, another set of issues. They are expected not to become personally committed to particular policy areas but rather to maintain objectivity by changing post every two or three years. This leads to a frustrating limit on corporate memory and on the ability of outside stakeholders to find the right person to contact on a particular matter. But if this practice is not followed and, for example, officials who have been involved since the emergence of the issue continue to work on the matter through Bill stage and became intimately involved in the substance of the policy issues and develop close working relationships with key stakeholders, there may come a point at which the Minister may find it difficult to accept advice from them as objective and impartial. For an individual Minister taking a Bill through Parliament is a high-risk activity and may mark the end instead of the hoped for advancement of his or her political career. But officials, though often hard-pressed and under pressure from many sources, are simply part of a team that shares responsibility and moves on to other matters.

Polish Legislative Procedure

To give a sharper perspective on the British legislative process, we will briefly describe some ways in which a Continental European system may differ. In Poland, as in other Continental European countries, constitutionally the President is directly elected by the population. The Prime

[16] Ibid.

Minister, as well as other ministers, may then be nominated from outside Parliament.[17] A government is often chosen to be a 'technical government' whereby the Prime Minister and his ministers are deliberately chosen from outside the political parties that are in opposition. Typically they include professors of law, economics or management who are asked to govern until a crisis resulting from the collapse of a ruling coalition is resolved and the party politicians return to rule.

Unlike the Westminster system wherein legislative initiatives in almost all cases come from government, in Poland the sources of legislation are more varied. The proportion of government initiatives has increased during successive terms since 1991, but Poland still clearly differs from the United Kingdom in the range of initiating actors. The President of the Republic has the right to initiate legislative process; but initiatives may also come from the legislative houses, that is, the Sejm committees, or from a group of at least 15 deputies in the Sejm, or from the Senate as a whole.[18] The Constitution also provides for the possibility of a popular initiative for law reform if a legislative draft is signed by at least 100,000 Polish citizens. This provision has been used only once. The Constitution on the one hand gives government the exclusive initiative in budgetary matters and, on the other hand, forbids it to propose any amendment to the Constitution.

There are legal departments in each ministry and a Governmental Legislative Centre (GLC) at the Prime Minister's office directly responsible for drafting, coordinating, checking cost implications and so on.[19] The law also says that the GLC must cooperate with the institutions of learning. The Centre is headed by a Director chosen by the Prime Minister from the civil arena and is required to cooperate with academic institutions. The Prime Minister is expected by law to 'define the elements of the methodology of preparation and ways of editing draft laws and other regulations, state the rules for preparing the reasons for the draft laws and for amending the law'.

If a law comes to Parliament from the government it always comes through the whole Council of Ministers and not from an individual minister or the Prime Minister. In the Sejm, the lower house, a draft goes through three readings, and amendments are proposed. When a draft is accepted it

[17] In Estonia, for example, the separation between executive and legislature is even clearer. If a member of Parliament becomes a member of the government, he or she must vacate the Parliamentary seat, which will be taken by the next candidate on the list for his or her party at the preceding election.

[18] In the last full term of Parliament (2001–05) out of 1265 legislative initiatives, almost 400 came directly from deputies.

[19] See Law on the Council of Ministers, 8 August 1996

becomes law but does not come into force, as it must be sent to the Senate, the upper house, which may reject it or, as frequently happens, introduce its own amendments and send the draft to the President, who may accept or veto it. Decisions of the Senate can be rejected by the Sejm but only with an absolute majority. The President will then usually sign the law and then send it to the Constitutional Court to check its constitutionality. If the Court finds it unconstitutional, the legislative process ends. Alternatively, the President may send it back to the Sejm, who then may vote on it again but need a majority of at least two thirds of votes to require the President to sign the law, which will then be published.

Government and Parliament have two sets of lawyers with strong senses of distinct identity; a representative of government may only take part in the work of a Parliamentary committee by invitation. But there are still confused lines of responsibility, as well as a lack of transparency and accountability. This is probably the result of the rapid way in which procedures have developed since 1989, as well as the fact that they are still changing. Moreoever, there is a long history of having no clear distinction between the role of politicians who are responsible for defining policy and that of the officials who are responsible for the technical tasks associated with putting it into legislative form.[20]

Comparison between the British and Polish systems of law-making reveal that Westminster embodies a more centralised legislative function, with a clearer pre-election agenda; tighter control by the ruling government of the legislative programme; and continuing importance of the independent professional civil service.

Case Studies in the Reform of English Family Law, 1989–2009

The areas we have chosen to discuss in detail represent a range of social issues, political aims and legislative outcomes. Family law in England and Wales has been a highly contentious and emotive area of legislative activity over the last twenty years, but with a strong and consistent focus

[20] These issues will be considered in more detail in the forthcoming companion volume to this book. Among other things, it will describe and analyse the 'Rywin Affair', in which attempts to reform the regulation of the media were confounded by the lack of clarity about the separation of responsibility and the differentiation of roles, particularly those of legal experts working within the media on the one hand and lawyers attached to the Government Legal Office who needed access to legal experts in media law on the other hand.

on promoting the interests of children. The legislative process has been supported by an experienced and knowledgeable team of officials at the Lord Chancellors Department (LCD), which later became the Department for Constitutional Affairs (DCA) and is now the Ministry of Justice (MoJ). Four statutes developed over a twenty-year period have been chosen for close examination: the Children Act 1989, the Child Support Act 1991, the Children and Adoption Act 2006 and the Children, Schools and Families Act 2010. We look at the stimulus to government to begin the legislative process in each case, the political and technical context and the progression of the law-making activity. We then turn to the outcome and ask whether the resulting statute was clear and enforceable; whether it was popular; and whether it accomplished what it set out to do or whether there were other unexpected outcomes. In addition, we ask what impact it has had on the further development of family law and policy? In sum, we investigate whether these legislative projects might be called successful.

In the first case study, presented in chapter two below, we describe the making of the Children Act (England and Wales) 1989, a highly regarded and enduring codification of the law relating to children. We suggest that the statute came into being with little political input or press comment; it was based on expert initiative and sound research evidence, and was worked on steadily without undue haste by a team of skilled policy officials and dedicated draftsmen. The Act was politically even-handed, giving paramountcy to the welfare of children in any matter relating to their care coming before the courts, thus pleasing those who sought strong powers to protect children, particularly in the wake of a number of very public tragic child deaths. At the same time the Act pleased those of more conservative views by requiring courts to show that no order was to be made unless it was clearly held to benefit the child. The lack of political interest in the passage of this legislation has been suggested by the key players involved in the law-making process as making a major contribution to its long-lasting and internationally emulated success.

In the second case study, presented in chapter three below, we tell a different story of a highly contentious and eventually repealed piece of legislation, the Child Support Act 1991. This statute was driven forward by a strong Prime Minster against the advice of experts and officials. In this case Prime Minister Margaret Thatcher took the view that since the divorce rate was increasing and more children were being left in poor circumstances following parental separation, the state should step in and require payment of a proportion of income from non-resident parents for the benefit of the children. This was a radical and robust public intervention in private life, yet it was carried through quickly and forcefully, effectively transferring matters that had previously received careful individual scrutiny in the family courts into the hands of an administrative agency. In the event, the Agency was ineffective and fell into disrepute. It has since been reformed with a less intrusive role under the Child Maintenance and Other Payments Act 2008 with the establishment of the Child Maintenance and Enforcement Commission (CMEC) now itself under review.

Where did the seeds of disaster lie with the Child Support Act? We will examine whether it was in the political imperative to do good and save public money through reducing the welfare bill; whether it was in the lack of skilled and patient handling; or whether it was in the lack of sound research into public attitudes and private resources. We will also consider whether there were positive aspects to the legislation, which were barely visible in the debris. In particular, the Act included provisions for all children of non-resident parents, whereas previous child maintenance systems provided little for children of unmarried separating parents.

The third case study, presented in chapter four below, addresses a legislative process strongly influenced by individuals, pressure groups and media interest. The Children and Adoption Act 2006 was prepared in response to the agitation of fathers' rights groups seeking more contact with their children after separation. The most extreme group, Fathers for Justice, wanted joint parenting, which they defined as an equal (fifty–fifty) division of a child's time between parents. This small but vociferous group led the campaign with daring exploits, such as scaling the Houses of Parliament and Buckingham Palace dressed as Batman and Robin. But we will argue that solid research input and a thoughtful team of officials helped to contain the movement, and Parliament finally upheld the major plank of the Children Act 1989, which states that in making any decision about the welfare and upbringing of a child, a court must have as its paramount consideration the welfare of that child. Even though the best interests of a child are hard to define, the Act concentrates attention on the needs of the child rather than the competing rights of the adults in dispute after separation or divorce. The welfare discourse has remained dominant in the face of strong challenges from the rights discourse, which has gained great prominence in the media. The outcome of the legislation has yet to become fully apparent, as implementation has been slow and limited in scope.

The final case study, presented in chapter five below, describes a legislative process in which the media played an even greater part, directly promoting their own interest in asking government to open up the family courts to achieve 'transparency'. But in this case the media interest was legitimated by being taken up by the Parliamentary body responsible for scrutiny of the justice system, the Constitutional Affairs Select Committee (CASC). The recommendation for increasing the openness of the family courts that came from the CASC in 2005 was an entirely appropriate source for legislative change. Sadly, the story of the Children, Schools and Families Act 2010 has not been a simple one of proper scrutiny – identifying problems, which government then addresses. We argue that the role of the media became strident and biased, and had a powerful effect on a Minister at a time of acute media criticism of an unpopular government facing an imminent general election.

The movement to make court processes more open was related to a campaign by fathers' groups to question the outcomes in contact cases in which they felt the courts were biased towards mothers. Some unfortunate child protection cases in which errors by expert witnesses led to inappropriate outcomes added to the public furore. In this context, the concerns of child and family organisations that making court processes transparent might violate individual privacy and might further strain family court resources were paid little heed. This is an interesting case of a media campaign leading to government action, and an example of the way in which proper processes can be affected or even subverted by the media and the political context. Although a thorough consultation had been undertaken by government, policy on the issue shifted direction significantly in the wake of press activity and changing ministerial responsibilities. The Bill that finally went to Parliament went much further towards meeting the demands of the press than earlier consultation documents published by the Department had led the public to expect. And it met considerable opposition as it passed through the Parliamentary process in the sensitive period immediately before the general election in 2010 at a time when government had urgent need to seek the support of the press.

What Constitutes Legislative Success?

As we worked through the case examples we also began to examine more carefully what led a law-making project to be regarded as a success or a failure, and these ideas are further developed below in the concluding chapter. But at this stage, we suggest that ideas about what might be thought a successful piece of law-making clearly depend on the viewpoint of those making the assessment. For the lawmakers there are a variety of criteria, and for government and the general public these range even wider. For legal draftsman we suggest success lies in the ability to set out clearly what is intended in such a way that it does not give rise to litigation requiring clarification from the courts. From an official's perspective, success might be thought to lie in the durability of the act and the ease of implementation. And from individual politicians' point of view success lies in the popularity of the legislation with the media and the electorate, particularly when an election is imminent. From our observations, to be developed below, the impact of public or political spotlight is certainly difficult to reconcile with an aim to develop detailed and effective legislative response to a perceived problem. The most successful piece of legislative activity that we discuss, the Children Act 1989, was clearly the Act of least interest to government, media or general public, but it was given lengthy and informed consideration by experts and practitioners.

Chapter six reviews the roles of the legislative actors and the balance of power between politicians inside and outside government; the officials who serve both Ministers and the public good; and lastly, the outside world of press and public. We look at the stimulus for legislative action in the form of political manifesto, Parliamentary scrutiny, independent review and consideration, and pressure group activity. We look at the political landscape for action and ask about the impact of a government's position on the legislative process: when is it in a strong enough position to attempt a difficult task, and when is it so defensive that it may seek symbolic projects to gain popularity? We then turn to the nature and purpose of each legislative task, whether it is to codify existing law, to withdraw unpopular regulation or to impose new demands on an unwilling public. Finally, to address our key question about what makes for successful legislation, we return to our original caveats about what law can and cannot do. A large part of success in the law-making process may yet be found to rest on understanding the art of the possible.

2

Successful Codification: The Making of the Children Act (England and Wales) 1989

Public and Private Family Law

FAMILY LAW IS always a difficult area for policymakers. The matters that require a regulatory framework involve individuals who are often distressed or angry, vulnerable parties who must be protected and a shortage of resources for providing advice or support either from the public purse through legal aid or for those needing to purchase help privately. The two key problems facing the justice system are delay and cost. The aim of the family law system is not to provide a social or welfare service but to offer fair and authoritative dispute management. As the Finer Report into the needs of one parents families said of the British family court in 1974:

> [I]t shall be a judicial institution which, in dealing with family matters, does justice according to law. The court must not see the man, woman or child with whom it is concerned as clients and still less as patients for whom the court process is just another kind of treatment. The individual in the family court must as remain the subject of rights and not the object of assistance.[1]

Sadly, dispute resolution may not be possible, even through adjudication when feelings run high and personalities are unlikely to change. Family law is always subject to criticism because it cannot make unhappy people happy, and it cannot satisfy the demands of all sections of a heterogeneous society in which many different values and expectations about family life are strongly held. At best it protects the vulnerable and supports informed negotiation and fair settlement.

[1] Committee on One-Parent Families, 'The Finer Report on One-Parent Families' (Cmnd 5629, 1974).

In England and Wales the common law system is made up of statutes supported by regulations, and judicial interpretation of these statutes provide clarification and set precedent.[2] This study focuses on the making of statute law and makes little reference to the impact of subsequent judicial interpretation. The impact of judicial interpretation is, however, again a matter of concern where it appears to depart from the original intentions of the legislator[3]

Family law is generally divided into two parts. Private law is concerned with disputes between individuals, for example, those involving the conduct of relationships between children and parents after divorce or separation and those surrounding the making of financial arrangements when one household divides into two. Public law, on the other hand, is concerned with disputes in which the state has a direct interest in protecting the vulnerable, whether they are adults involved in domestic violence or children at risk of neglect or abuse. In public law, the state faces the problem of how to protect a child and at the same time protect the human rights of the parents to privacy and family life. If public intervention comes too rarely or too late children will suffer. If it comes too often or too early the parents can claim that their rights are not being respected. Although this distinction between public and private law is clearly defined and carries with it different procedures and remedies, nevertheless the problems that come before the courts often affect people experiencing the same kinds of difficult family circumstances. A case may move from private to public law if, for example, there is a dispute over the contact a child will have with a non-resident father (a private law matter), and then allegations are made by at mother about child abuse or violence in the home (a public law matter).

Legislative responses to a variety of family law matters are often requested by interest groups and think-tanks, who ask for anything from removing all state intervention in family life to tightening controls over behaviour in the home, particularly violent behaviour. Choosing which issues from the many requests put to Ministers to address through legislation is the task of Government. Getting the policy right and clearly set out is a multidisciplinary task, best undertaken gradually and outside the glare of party political interest. Setting the policy in law is the responsibility of

[2] Scotland has a different system that is closer to the civil systems of Continental Europe, and Scots family law is now a devolved matter that is dealt with by the Scottish Parliament.

[3] See P Harris and R George, 'Parental Responsibility and Shared Residence Orders: Parliamentary Intentions and Judicial Interpretations' (2010) 22(2) *Child and Family Law Quarterly* 151.

legal draftsmen, and once set the law becomes the 'medium for the message'.[4]

As we described in chapter one, this volume looks at four pieces of legislation, which, though all dealing with family matters, represent an extraordinary range of contexts, aims, process and outcomes – from which we will develop a typology of legislative action. The most recent case, still without a commencement date at the time of writing is the Children, Schools and Families Act 2010, which deals with many matters pertaining to education that are beyond the scope of this analysis but also includes measures to increase the access of the media to family courts. This is a most unusual piece of legislation in that it can be interpreted as both blatant courting of press support in the period leading to the General Election early in 2010, but it can also be seen as an idealistic attempt to free the family justice system from out-dated secrecy and the associated suspicions about bias or incompetence. Pressure for action followed paternal disquiet about parenting issues after separation , compounded by errors in expert witness statements in a small number of high profile child protection cases. The subsequent media campaign, which will be discussed further in chapter 5, led to Government interest and a lengthy period of careful consultation about how to balance openness and transparency with the need to protect the privacy of those involved in these distressing cases, particularly the children. A four year period of consultation resulted in the shift of emphasis away from inviting the press in to court, and towards making sure that clear anonymised information about the decisions taken in such cases could be posted on a website (as is the case in Scotland) . However, a change of minister and a determined press campaign by an individual journalist who won a prize for the work led to a speedy change in policy direction and the introduction of a bill which offers the press far greater access to court hearing and documents that is the case in any other jurisdiction. This has led to widespread anxiety and the future of the bill hung in the balance as a bitterly contested election got closer, finally being dealt with in the last days before parliamentary dissolution. So, with its origins in error and anxiety, but also a careful consultation process, the pressure of a forthcoming election appears to have driven forward a hasty and ill conceived piece of legislation.

The case study preceding this final one looks at the Children and Adoption Act 2006 dealing with contact and residence i.e. private law dis-

[4] This phrase was often used by John Gasson, Legal Adviser to the Lord Chancellor during the passage of the Children Act 1989 [personal communication].

putes between parents, which was also affected by high profile media interests this time in the idiosyncratic activities of troubled individuals. During the 1990s there was a surge across many jurisdictions of pressure from fathers who believed that they were being prevented from having enough time with their children after separation to enable them to support an ongoing meaningful relationship. This will be discussed in depth in chapter 4. But although the antics of some of the parties led to considerable media sympathy, (for example, climbing up to the face of Big Ben at Westminster, and scaling the walls of Buckingham Palace to draw attention to their problem) the government took time to examine the research evidence with care, and came to the conclusion that each child's case should be examined on its merits, and found no reason to depart from the welfare paramountcy principle in the Children Act 1989 which makes the best interests of the child the court's paramount concern in making any decision concerning that child and its upbringing. Perhaps the large parliamentary majority, the absence of an imminent election, and a firm knowledge base helped to make it easier to take a balanced view.

The events examined in the two earlier case studies were of far less interest to the popular press. The Child Support Act 1991 (repealed and replaced in 2008) attempted to deal with the intractable problem of the private responsibility of non-resident parents to contribute financially to the care of their children . But the legislative activity in this case arose directly from the wishes of the then Prime Minister Margaret Thatcher, who was outraged to discover that, at a time of financial stringency and the need to cut public expenditure, men who had left a first family were able to rely on the state to support them while going on to form a new family with a second partner. The first piece of legislation we will discuss, the Children Act of 1989, brought public and private law together in a coherent synthesis. It has been universally admired both in this country and internationally, and moreover has stood the test of time. 'The Children Act 20 years on' is becoming a common headline. We therefore begin with this success story and will try to identify the factors associated with its success.

The Children Act (England and Wales) 1989

In introducing the Children Bill to Parliament the then Lord Chancellor Lord Mackay described it as 'the most comprehensive and far-reaching' legislation on children 'in living memory'.[5] The legal historian Stephen Cretney characterised this acclaim, with typical English reticence, as 'not a significant exaggeration'.[6]

Professor Cretney has provided a clear and full account of the events that led up to calls for law reform. There had been reports in the 1980s from inquiries into the deaths of Jasmine Beckford and Kimberley Carlisle, children who had slipped through the net of responsible agencies and tragically lost their lives at the hands of those caring for them. Subsequently there had been widespread concern about unfounded allegations of networks of child abusers, particularly in Cleveland, which demonstrated the existing system's failure to protect both vulnerable children and innocent parents. The complex web of statute, precedent and regulation was becoming unmanageable. An uncomfortable 'family values' or 'state versus family' debate was beginning between those who followed the principle of non-intervention in family life and those who urged the state to be proactive in supporting the welfare of children. The case of Victoria Gillick, who objected to the provision of contraceptive advice to her teenage daughter by the National Health Service (NHS),[7] added fuel to the flames. The law relating to children was complex and in many instances unclear, and in urgent need of codification.

The public process of reform began with the reports of Parliamentary committees that oversee the work of individual government departments. These Select Committees are appointed for a whole Parliament and tend to become expert on their subject matter. Party political differences become less important as time passes, and there is usually a good degree of consensus. The Committees are accorded considerable respect. In 1984 the Second Report of the Social Services Committee, known as the Short Committee Report[8], recommended 'a thorough review of the body of statute law, regulation and judicial decisions relating to children with a view to . . . a simplified and coherent body of law comprehensible to . . . those operating it . . . and to those affected by its operation'. They further recommended that the review should be carried out by a working party made up of lawyers, social workers and others, under the direction of the Department of Health and subject to a tight timetable to produce a draft code of child law within nine months.

[5] Lord Mackay of Clashfern, LC, Official Report (HL) vol 502,col489.

[6] S Cretney, *Family Laws in the Twentieth Century* (Oxford, Oxford University Press, 2003).

[7] *Gillick v West Norfolk and Wisbech Area Health Authority* [1986] AC 112 HL.

[8] Second Report from the Social Services Committee, Session 1983–84, Children in Care, Vol 1 (HC 360-1,1984)

An Interdepartmental Working Party on the Care of Children (IDWP) was duly created that year to set out options for the codification and amendment of public child care law; it included representatives of the Department of Health and Social Security, the Lord Chancellor's Department, the Home Office and the Law Commission. At the same time the Law Commission, the independent body charged by Government with considering law reform, announced that it would review private child law. The Working Party published 12 discussion papers over the course of 1985. The Law Commission published its first consultation paper on private child law in 1985, followed by its final consultation paper in 1987. 'Review of Child Law, Guardianship and Custody' followed in 1989, with draft statutory clauses demonstrating how a comprehensive code of public as well as private child law might be achieved, excluding only adoption.

This series of reports was interspersed with inquiries into a number of tragic incidents. A report into the death of Kimberley Carlisle was published in 1987, and the Inquiry into Child Abuse in Cleveland in 1988 found that paediatricians and social workers there had been over zealous in identifying cases of abuse.

The Children Bill was introduced into Parliament in the House of Lords by the Lord Chancellor in autumn 1988 and received the Royal Assent, becoming law in autumn 1989. It has remained in force, scarcely amended, to the present day – an unusual lifespan for a matter of family regulation in a period of such rapid changes in family life and family values. The legislative process had taken five years. A programme of systematic evaluation of its impact was subsequently carried out by the Department of Health and the findings widely disseminated.[9]

As we have described briefly above, Parliament is the law-making body, amending and subsequently assenting to the legislative proposals laid before it by the Government of the day. But the purpose of this account is to look behind the Parliamentary curtain to the work of the bodies mentioned above, to add the private to the public history of the Children Act. We were fortunate in being able to add to our own memories of this process by holding a seminar in Oxford in May 2006 at which the key players – Ministers, officials, Law Commissioners and Parliamentary draftsman – came together to discuss what had happened and how the Act came to be such a well-regarded and long-lived statutory intervention. This section draws on the excellent account of that seminar prepared for the group by Peter Harris and published in the journal *Family Law*.[10]

[9] See, for example, Lord Justice Thorpe and C Cowton (eds), *Delight and Dole: The Children Act 10 Years On* (Bristol, Family Law, 2002).

[10] P Harris, 'The Children Act: A Private History' (2006) 36 *Family Law* 1054.

At the Oxford seminar, chaired by Maclean, those taking part emphasised a number of factors that were thought to have contributed to the success of the Children Act. Foremost among these was the unusual degree of continuity in the core team of law-workers throughout the five years of policy definition and preparation of the legislation. Rupert Hughes, the Assistant Secretary at the Department of Health and Social Security (DHSS), the official responsible for policy development, chaired the IDWP and stayed on to lead the team of officials charged with preparing the Bill for Parliament. He was advised throughout by Robert Aitken, the DHSS lawyer responsible for child protection law, and by the chief adviser on social services, Wendy Rose. Baroness Brenda Hale (subsequently to be the first lady Law Lord and now a member of the Supreme Court) was then a Law Commissioner and distinguished academic family lawyer. She not only led the work of the Commission but was also a member of the IDWP and later acted as a ministerial adviser during the Parliamentary stages of the Bill. In addition, several of the key people involved moved into Whitehall to take forward the legislation in Parliament: Sir Edward Caldwell, who drafted the clauses for the Law Commission; Jonathan Whybrow and Peter Harris, who were members of the Law Commission Family Law Team; and the analysts who helped the IDWP. Caldwell returned to Whitehall as Parliamentary Counsel and was the Government's Parliamentary draftsman on the Bill. Whybrow joined the DHSS Bill team as a policy adviser, and Harris moved back to the Lord Chancellor's department (LCD), where he led the team on the Children Bill and became the Assistant Secretary responsible for Family Law.

At the seminar it became clear that the bringing together of the Law Commission with government policymakers in the IDWP was initiated by the then Secretary to the Law Commission and later LCD Legal Adviser, John Gasson, who had a strong interest in procedural and accessible justice. The IDWP maintained good contact with all the relevant 'stakeholders', both professionals and interest groups, throughout the review period, issuing lengthy and well researched papers for consultation and entering into close consultation with groups such as the British Association for Fostering and the Children's Rights Centre. There were discussions about who should be representing children; about the human rights issues in disputes about contact between children in the care of the local authority and their parents; and about how children were taken into care. Were social workers snatching children away from innocent parents or delaying until lives were at risk? The debate was active and inevitably emotionally charged. It continues to this day, with the intervention of the Barnardo's

Charity in August 2010 demanding that welfare authorities should take action earlier to protect children from abuse or harm.[11]

Meanwhile, academic research in the field was developing rapidly, some commissioned by Government and also by the Economic and Social Research Council (ESRC), notably the empirical socio-legal work undertaken in Oxford by John Eekelaar and Robert Dingwall with Topsy Murray on child protection.[12] This team looked closely at the new procedures followed in medical settings, as well as at those used by local authority social services departments; and they interviewed professionals in both settings. Their considered view was that local authorities followed the golden rule of optimism, believing the best of families until compelled to believe that a child is in danger of neglect or abuse. As they pointed out, no hard-pressed social services department had the resources to take on unnecessary work and had every incentive to believe parents. When they did take action, however, it was highly unlikely to be an unnecessary intervention.

This careful research was a powerful voice in the public debate, which included a great deal of anxiety about the apparent shift in policy emphasis away from parental rights and towards the importance of professional action to defend the welfare of children (which was of course to be defined by these same professionals). The reorganisation of local government social services in 1970 had produced large and powerful organisations, against which a parent might feel powerless. At the same time, however, there were concerns about the 'verbal abuse of social workers bordering on the hysterical in the popular press', and social workers were finding it difficult to cope with threats of violence and 'saturation media coverage devoted to each child abuse case'.[13]

Against this background of highly charged if not party political debate, a new culture of openness and discussion between policy officials, lawyers , practitioners and the research community developed and continued throughout the period. This was of great value in enhancing the quality of the law-making work. The continuity was seen by participants in the Oxford seminar as vital to the quality of the resultant policy and legislation; it ensured the build-up of expertise, common understandings and consensus between the key players and between the government departments involved and the Law Commission.

[11] Martin Neary, *The Observer*, 8 August 2010.

[12] R Dingwall, J Eekelaar and T Murray, *The Protection of Children: State Intervention and Family Life* (Avebury, Aldershot, 1995).

[13] London Borough of Greenwich, 'A Child in Mind: Protection of Children in a Responsible Society', report into the circumstances surrounding the death of Kimberly Carlisle (1987).

The seminar in Oxford was held under the Chatham House convention that views may be repeated but not attributed without permissions. The view of the meeting was that the quality of any legislation is as dependent on the competence of the team formulating the policy as on the drafting skills of Parliamentary counsel. In the British civil service tradition the emphasis on the generic skills of public servants, combined with a requirement to be flexible and not remain for more than two or three years in a specific job, can lead to a lack of in-depth understanding of any single policy area – though the argument is also made that staying too long in a particular area of work leads to the development of vested interests and a loss of objectivity. In the case of the Children Act the continuity added to the depth of understanding, but officials were protected from any undesirable overinvestment in a particular viewpoint by the breadth and openness of their discussions both within and outside the confines of Whitehall.

The continuity was also seen as efficient in that it avoided the need to spend time and energy on renegotiating or refighting old battles with new arrivals on the team, or simply to bring new arrivals up-to-date. While some members of the team felt that more project management might have been helpful, it was agreed at the Oxford seminar that the need to divert resources to management was greatly reduced by the shared understanding and 'professional intimacy' enjoyed by the key players. Indeed, as the chair of the seminar, Maclean was delighted by the pleasure that this group of colleagues expressed at the prospect of meeting again ten years after working together – and indeed how well they worked together throughout the seminar itself.

The seminar also made apparent the wide range of experience, knowledge, skills and approaches of the key players involved in the creation of the Children Act. Baroness Hale was at the time not only a family law specialist but also an academic who had written widely on public and child law. Wendy Rose was a social services expert. Robert Aitken had acted for the government in European Court of Human Rights litigation challenging public law. Edward Caldwell was a senior and influential draftsman, while Rupert Hughes and Peter Harris were 'Whitehall warriors' with an understanding and knowledge of government and departmental machinery.

Differences of approach, which in a less collegiate environment might have resulted in less than coherent compromises, were remembered by the players as enriching the policy. For example, while some gave high priority to the privacy and integrity of the family unit and were wary of intervention by the courts or other state authorities save as a last resort, others took a more positive view of the help the state might offer to families and children in need. The result was the development of a legal code that brought together lawyerly concerns about human rights with social-service based policy objectives. Rules were explicitly formulated to protect families from meddling courts and local authorities but at the same time aimed to empower the organs of the state to act vigorously and flexibly to promote the interests of vulnerable children. At a more personal level, the Seminar recalled how some players were dynamic and creative in driving policy forward and how others, while no less committed, brought cool judgement to keep policy balanced, well-founded and on track.

This team spirit encouraged and enabled individuals to work across professional boundaries. The traditional Whitehall demarcation between policymakers (the officials and civil servants who advise Ministers), departmental lawyers (who give professional advice to the policy makers) and the Parliamentary Counsel (who convert policy into statutory form under instructions from these departmental lawyers) were ignored. Lawyers delved into policy formation, and policy advisers dealt directly with Parliamentary Counsel in a process of personal and professional interaction, which all saw as enriching the resolution of policy issues. The flexibility of roles resulted no doubt in part from the involvement of the Law Commission, where lawyers traditionally formulate policy. But it was also encouraged by the non-lawyers on the team who believed that the legal analysis and close involvement of the lawyers and draftsmen were crucial in teasing out the policy issues and formulating proposals for reform.

The close and effective relationship between policymakers and legal draftsmen meant that the lawyers did not have the frustration of attempting to draft precise terms for an imprecise policy, and the policymakers likewise had assistance in encapsulating a complex issue in clear legal terms. Nonetheless, there were of course problems in getting a place in the legislative programme. When difficulties arose about getting a place in the House of Commons timetable, a White Paper was produced as a kind of holding action, stating government aims and plans. This was drafted with the agreement that any bill would not contain more than 80 clauses, and no additional public expenditure would be required when the bill came into effect. The latter point could be defended on the basis that most of the costs that might ensue would arise through local authorities carrying out work which they were already meant to be doing but had not been doing recently. This line attracted sympathy in the aftermath of the Cleveland Inquiry into child sexual abuse. The restriction on the number of clauses, however, was problematic – the team wanted around 150 clauses but was required to work within a limit of 80 clauses. In the event, Parliamentary Counsel skilfully prepared a Bill that had only 79 clauses, but many of these clauses carried a large number of lengthy attached schedules, a solution that would have been unlikely to happen had it not been for the high level of commitment and cooperation that characterised the Bill team. The Bill grew as it went through Parliament, as none of the work on repeals of earlier legislation had been done in advance. There was some regret that adoption could not be dealt with at the same time to complete the codification of child-related law; but there was great benefit in the continuing discussion between Law Commission and Lord Chancellor's Department.

So far we have discussed the making of the Children Act in terms of the work of experts, policymakers and lawyers. Politicians, government ministers and Parliament have scarcely been mentioned, as the entire process was very apolitical. Government, in the form of the second Thatcher administration, had not sought a particular piece of legislation but accepted that there was a need to consider the legal machinery for the protection of children in response to public concerns. The referral of the issue to the Law Commission guaranteed a careful and considered response rather than knee-jerk policymaking or purely symbolic legislation. Ministers were not heavily involved. The press gave a great deal of coverage to the tragic incidents but did not call for a 'quick fix', recognising the complexity of the issues. This lack of ministerial attention enabled officials to work without the distortions that arise from party political pressures. Indeed, the spirit of cooperation and open discussion extended to Parliamentary circles, and there were meetings between Government and members of Parliament from the opposition parties to take the work forward.

One other apparent problem turned out in the event to provide a positive opportunity. There was no Parliamentary time available for more than one Bill, so instead of working towards two bills, one for public and one for private child law, the team attempted to address both areas in the one Bill. This had the benefit of requiring the team to take a fresh approach to the issues, starting from scratch. For example, the previous private law position that there was no need for the courts to interfere if the parents were agreed about what they wanted to do was taken over into public law, with the caveat of respect for the best interests of the child. There could easily have been a less coherent codification if the Bill had been divided into two.

As well as a culture of openness and cooperation, the Children Act was prepared in a culture of innovation and ambition. The exercise broke not only traditional demarcation boundaries but also many of the other 'rules' that surround the way the Law Commission and Whitehall were accustomed to working. Sir John Gasson, then Secretary to the Commission, was aware that the Commission was seen by some in Government as a sideshow, with unimplemented reports piling up on dusty shelves. With encouragement from then Permanent Secretary (the most senior civil servant) at LCD Sir Thomas Legg, Gasson saw his task as making the Commission more relevant and central to Government's needs. He seized the opportunity to persuade the Commissioners to make their expertise and resources available to the IDWP, a step that traditionalists at the time saw as dangerous because it might compromise the independence of the Commission and would furthermore involve using scarce Commission resources to do what was essentially the government's work. The Bill was definitely branded as a government initiative.

But the exercise both coincided with and drove innovation within the Law Commission. In addition to having a Commissioner join an interdepartmental working party and later act as a ministerial adviser, and in addition to providing a legal analysis team to the IDWP, the exercise drew in one of the first research assistants ever appointed by the Commission, Jonathan Whybrow.

Ambition, innovation and a willingness to cross traditional boundaries is also apparent in the fact that while the IDWP was tasked by Ministers only with identifying options for codifying and amending child law, it came back with 233 detailed proposals for fundamental reform. And while the Commission's review was limited to private law, it exploited its statutory powers to promote the simplification, modernisation and codification of the law to include in that review a draft Bill setting out the basics of a unified code, which also reflected Government's proposals on public law and formed the basis of what became the Children Act 1989.

This spirit of innovation and thoughtful irreverence for established procedure can be seen during the passage of the Bill through parliament. As we have noted, the restriction on the number of clauses was managed through the creativeness of Parliamentary Counsel through strategic use of schedules. Instructions to Parliamentary Counsel tend to come in stages, and drafting is an organic process. The overall story emerges slowly, and the final shape of a bill becomes visible only towards the end of the process. The focus tends to be on macro policy, but the devil is in the detail. The sooner Parliamentary Counsel are involved and the closer their interest in the matter, the more effectively the mass of detailed decisions at the micro level can be taken. For example, Treasury concerns about additional public expenditure were met by showing in detail how the Bill would impose no new duties on local authorities, even though those authorities were not currently discharging their existing duties in part due to the lack of clarity and the weakness in the existing law, which the Bill was designed to address. It is unlikely that Treasury would have been convinced by any less specific briefing from policy officials. The innovative spirit even affected Ministers in Parliament, who quite remarkably gave Opposition members direct and unsupervised access to the Bill team and draftsmen to discuss issues arising and potential amendments.

The team dynamics and spirit of trust and challenge, together with the need to 'dig up the foundations' of the public and private child law in order to create a coherent code seem to have encouraged innovation in policy formation. For example, the Bill disposed of a set of family disputes centred on parental rights by ceasing to use the term 'rights' and turning instead to the concept of parental obligation. Formerly, disputes about custody and access after divorce had been set out in terms that seemed to treat the child almost as another piece of marital property to be disposed of. The new Bill, however, refocused the attention and the powers of the courts on the more practical issue of where a child would be living and who would be in contact with the child in the case of dispute. If there was no dispute, there need be no order. Indeed, an order should not be made unless it would be of benefit to the child. If there were other specific issues to be resolved these could be the subject of an order. Any matter could be reopened: custody was no longer to be awarded as quasi-ownership of the child.

The Bill also held the seeds of a unified family jurisdiction after years of failed attempts to set up a family court. In child protection the criteria for taking a child into care were set out clearly as a purposive welfare checklist, identifying the needs of the child to be met by a local authority through its care plan, rather than being symptom- based and backward-looking. There was to be no possibility of a local authority being given responsibility for the care of a child unless there was clear evidence that the child was in danger of abuse or neglect. The welfare checklist must be applied, and the safety threshold passed before intervention in the form of a care plan can come into play, thus making a neat division between forensic inquiry and treatment plan. The lines of responsibility were clarified between executive (local authority) and judicial powers (the courts) by reconciling the statutory powers to protect children with the prerogative and common law powers of the Crown, exercised through wardship proceedings in the High Court.

As Cretney and others have noted, the Children Act, in failing to embrace adoption law, was not as comprehensive as some might have wished. Those involved in developing the policy within government, while accepting the criticism and sharing the disappointment, point to it as demonstrating a sense of realism without which the whole enterprise might have failed. They see a sharp sense of what is achievable in practice as being as important as ambition and vision in driving through major reforms. In particular, they feel it would have been rash to postpone legislating when the opportunity presented itself in 1988, given the limitations of resources, including Parliamentary time, and increasing risks to maintaining a consensus as the policy agenda expanded and time ran on. The broader the coverage, the greater the likelihood of a division between the family-protectors and the child-savers. Competent policy development and legislation, like politics, appear to be the art of the possible.

The team's internal culture of openness and the value placed on challenge and consensus, together with the continuity of personnel, are remembered by the team as enabling relationships to develop between team members and the various stakeholders within and outside Whitehall, including the judiciary and professional and other interest groups. Those relationships were essential not just in ensuring that the team had access to the views of those on the ground but also as a means of developing and maintaining general consent and commitment to the policies. This in due course provided the foundation for the perceived success of the implementation of the Act. For example, only a forward-looking and committed family judiciary would have willingly accepted the new specialist training requirement that accompanied commencement of the legislation, which was part of a general move away from the courts' traditional adjudicatory function towards a more investigatory and managed approach to cases.

It was suggested at the Oxford seminar that the consensus also helped to avoid party political conflict and interdepartmental competition, which in turn relieved career pressure on Ministers and freed them to accept the advice coming from the team and those in the field. In that sense the Bill can be seen to be the product of technocrats rather than politicians, both in the team and on the ground, be they social workers, judges, lawyers or charities. What we may then term the 'consensus technocratic approach' was reflected in the Parliamentary stages, with the Bill, as a Government measure, being introduced and handled in the House of Lords by Lord Chancellor Mackay. His constitutional position, apolitical background and reputation for fairness and sound judgment were remembered as facilitating a cross-party consensus that one key player pointed out complied with an earlier Lord Chancellor's edict that law reform must be 'by consent or not at all'. Indeed some participants in the seminar recalled proposals for amendments to the policy or the Bill being withdrawn because the proposers accepted that while their suggestion had merit, they were unlikely to be able to improve on the conclusions reflected in the Bill given the independent input of the Law Commission and the support of the extra-Parliamentary stakeholders.

This unusually positive account of the legislative process has led some of those involved to speculate on the part played by luck in the perceived success of the Bill. One could point to the coincidental release of the Government's response to the Short Committee Report, Brenda Hale's appointment to the Law Commission and a Commission Secretary determinedto develop a new role for the organisation. In addition, the constant stream of official reports into the deaths and alleged abuse of children gave the policy impetus and sustainability, securing it a legislative slot despite the absence of any party political imperative. There was also the luxury of having four years to produce a Bill, which allowed for the policy options to be thoroughly considered and consulted on. Finally, there was the serendipitous mix of individuals in the team who remain firm friends twenty years on, as well as the continuity achieved through the return of Commission-based staff to jobs in Whitehall, which maintained their involvement.

Certainly there do seem to have been favourable coincidences and lucky breaks, including the quality of the Ministers who had responsibility for the bill. But these lucky breaks were in fact opportunities that had to be seized. The four years that might be seen as offering time for relaxed policy work are remembered by the key players as a period of intense activity and pressure to carry out research and extend the scope of the policy work. Those who moved into Whitehall from the Commission were active in bidding for jobs that would keep them involved, some (Aitken and Whybrow) even giving up the chance of professional advancement to remain involved. And it was the vision and commitment of John Gasson and Brenda Hale that locked the independent Commission into the governmental legislative process. It is hard to ignore the role of the zeal and enterprise of the key players in identifying and maximising the opportunities that presented themselves.

Although the matter did not become a party political issue, there were serious and distressing conflicts among those dealing with children about whether parental rights were being ridden over roughshod and whether excessive power was being given to the social work profession, which was still recovering from the criticisms of recent inquiries. For example, the Cleveland Report had described how the police had ceased to cooperate with paediatricians and social workers as they simply did not believe the allegations being made. But the team managed to stand outside this debate and strike a successful balance between those seeking to protect the autonomy of the family and those prioritising child protection. The Government of the day, conservative in its orientation towards family values, could maintain that the Act upholds the view that the best place for a child is in the family, with both parents playing a full part. But when a child is at risk, the Act is unequivocal, though requiring any intervention to be sanctioned by the court. As Lord Mackay said,

> Unless there is evidence that a child is being or is likely to be positively harmed because of failure of the family, the State, whether in the guise of a local authority should not interfere . . . [T]he integrity of the family is the basic building block of a free and democratic society, and the need to defend it should be clearly perceivable in the law . . . [T]o provide otherwise would make it lawful for children to be removed from their families simply on the basis that a court considers the state could do better for the child than his family. The threat to poor and minority groups whose views of what is good for a child may not coincide closely with that of the majority is all too apparent . . .[14]

Concluding Observations

Legislative reform is only as good as the policy work it reflects and gives life to. The enduring quality of what Cretney has called 'a superb piece of legal machinery, not only codification of procedure but the making of a coherent and socially binding intellectual and moral approach' was heavily dependent on those involved, who prioritised the following:

- the formation and maintenance of a core team to handle the work from its inception to its completion, including early and continuing involvement by departmental lawyers and draftsmen;
- the inclusion of experts from outside Whitehall who had the required mix of skills, knowledge and experience as well as personal qualities that complemented each other and as a group were able to work together in a way that encouraged constructive debate and innovation but ultimately fostered consensus;
- the crossing of functional, institutional and professional boundaries within the government machinery;

[14] Lord Mackay (1989) *New Law Journal* 505–07.

- thorough and relevant research on which to base policy, as well as systematic analysis of all proposed project plans;
- consensus between departments, Ministers and extra-Whitehall stakeholders; and
- a balance between ambition and vision on the one hand and a sense of realism about what can be achieved within the limits of time and other prevailing constraints on the other hand.

These conclusions may look like bland statements of what management consultants would consider to be the obvious necessary elements for a successful project. What is remarkable and disappointing, as Peter Harris has pointed out, is that the key players at the Oxford seminar saw their experience on this legislative project as wholly exceptional. It suggests either that the obvious requirements are often ignored by those responsible for setting up and running law-making projects or that it is difficult or even impossible for them to work on that basis given the realities of life in government – where the events and the political realities tend to determine who does what, when and how, rather than the dictates of good practice and effective project working.

Furthermore, it might be suggested that the perceived success of the Children Act had much to do with the nature of the task. Codification may be inherently more consensual than imposing new requirements or regulation. And as to the content, how could the welfare of children be a party political issue? Or perhaps the way it was handled was only possible because the topic was naturally susceptible to widespread consensus? But it should be remembered that the degree to which it is acceptable for the state to intervene in family life raises fundamental questions of political philosophy and ideology, around which there is still no true consensus. In this case, we suggest it was the way the exercise was handled that made it possible to contain the potential for conflict and avoid damage to the law-making exercise.

To understand better both this issue and the extent to which the priorities listed above may be more or less soundly based, we need to look at a second example of law-making, the case of the Child Support Act 1991 (which will be discussed in the following chapter). Here, too, many of the personnel remained the same and the issue was closely concerned with the welfare of children in troubled families – but the outcome was regarded as far from successful.

Sadly, the limitations of even excellent law-making continued to become apparent as the stream of scandals about children suffering at the hands of their parents before the Children Act was followed afterwards by tragic accounts of the suffering of children in the hands of those working in the services set up to help them, including Sir Ronald Waterhouse's Report into sexual abuse in a children's home in North Wales.[15] And in Sir John Utting's report 'People Like Us', the Secretary of State declared:

> [M]any children who had been taken into care to protect and help them had not been protected and helped. Instead some had suffered abuse at the hands of those who were meant to help them. Many more had been let down, never given the attention they needed, shifted from place to place, school to school, and turned out when they reached 16. The whole system had failed.[16]

Using medical parlance, we might say that the operation was a success, but the patient died.

At the time of writing (February 2011) the Ministry of Justice is completing a fundamental review of the family justice system. While questioning all aspects of court process and governance, as well as the roles of the professionals involved in family matters, in its terms of reference it nevertheless stands by the child-centredness of the Children Act 1989. But as always, even clear, thoughtful consensual codification of the law can only achieve what is achievable by law.

Issues about delay and cost in the system remain and are being addressed at the time of writing by the Family Justice Review, which is unlikely to find easy solutions. In 2010, as in 1989, there may be a desire to push back to the welfare sector work that has slipped across to the courts, such as the need to examine a threshold statement in detail instead of accepting a social worker's report, and examining instead of accepting local authority care plans. However, these are matters of the availability of resources and good standards in management and practice. The legal framework remains eminently fit for purpose.

[15] R Waterhouse, 'Report of the Tribunal of Enquiry into the Abuse of Children in Care in the Former County Council Areas of Gwynedd and Clwyd since 1974' (The Waterhouse Report) (HC 1999–2000).

[16] Sir William Utting 'People Like Us': the Report on the Review of Safeguards for Children Living Away from Home Department of Health/Welsh Office, 1997.

3

Prime Ministerial Intervention: The Child Support Act 1991

THE CHILD SUPPORT Act of 1991 attempted to enforce the financial responsibility of parents (mainly fathers) who do not live with their children. The legislation did not enjoy the long and internationally acclaimed life of the Children Act, which was passed two years earlier. There were early reviews and revisions in the face of immediate and continuing criticism, and by 2006 public loss of confidence in the child support system had reached such a low point that the then Prime Minister Tony Blair asked Sir David Henshaw to review the running of the child support scheme.

The Child Support Agency had been set up to ensure that non-resident parents make appropriate financial contributions to their children's upbringing, both in the case of separation or divorce and when parents had never shared a joint home. Sir David concluded in his report *Recovering Child Support: Routes to Responsibility*, published in July 2006 that the Child Support Agency set up by the 1991 legislation was 'not fit for purpose' and should be replaced.[1] The level of uncollected child support had remained unchanged and is still high;[2] the Agency was taking far too long to make assessments; and many resident parents, especially those in receipt of welfare payments, were seeing little benefit.

In this chapter we will look behind the scenes at the making of this legislation, which is widely perceived to have been unsuccessful. We will not discuss in any detail here the recent reforms that led to the Child Maintenance and Other Payments Act 2008, which resulted in greater powers to enable the Child Support Agency to collect arrears but at the

[1] D Henshaw, *Recovering Child Support: Routes to Responsibility* (The Henshaw Report) (Department of Work and Pensions, July 2006) Cm 6894.

[2] The level of unpaid arrears was stated to be £3,761 million on 12 July 2010, in response to a Parliamentary Question from Natascha Engel, MP.

same time will probably mean that more private arrangements will be made.[3]

As with the Children Act 1989, which was discussed in the previous chapter, we had the benefit of personal involvement in the making of with the Child Support Act. In 1989 Maclean was appointed as an academic consultant to the Interdepartmental Working Group chaired by Peter Harris which was set up to look into child maintenance, and worked under Harris with a desk within the Lord Chancellor's Department (LCD). This section also draws on discussion at the second Oxford Seminar on the legislative process, which was held in November 2007. At that meeting, key players in the 1991 Act – including Ministers, senior civil servants, legal advisers, draftsmen, stakeholder groups including One Parent Families who worked closely with government , and representatives from the Prime Minister's Policy Unit – came together to discuss the development of the Act.

Why is the outcome of the legislative process that led to the Child Support Act generally perceived to be so much less successful than that of the Children Act? There are a number of apparent similarities in the social and policy contexts that might lead us to expect a similarly successful outcome. An important issue had been identified, arising from the increasing separation between parenting and partnering. The increasing rate of divorce and marital separation had led to a rise in the number of children living in poverty in one-parent families. This in turn put pressure on the public welfare funds required for their support. Government sought an effective policy that could deal with both these issues – that is, alleviate child poverty and trim public expenditure – neither of which were themselves contentious. The Conservative government at the time was led by a strong Prime Minster, Margaret Thatcher. There were competent and well-informed people working on the Bill, including a number of those who had worked on the Children Act (for example, Peter Harris, who was in charge of Family Policy at the Lord Chancellor's Department, and Edward Caldwell, who acted as Parliamentary Counsel). Why was the outcome of this law-making project so different?

[3] For a full account, see B Fehlberg and M Maclean, 'Child Support Policy in Australia and the UK: Changing Priorities but a Similar Tough Deal for Children' (2009) 23(1) *International Journal of Law, Policy and the Family.*

Background

Despite the 1969 introduction of no-fault divorce in the United Kingdom, financial arrangements on divorce for a long time had the appearance of being merely an extension of the marital dispute. The greater part of the disposal of resources available for transfer between men and women were discussed under the heading of spousal support, although research carried out in the early 1980s had shown that money moved between households almost always only when there were children of the marriage involved.[4] 'Pure' spousal support was rare, although it was common for courts to make orders either for a wife, or for any child, or for any wife and children together, depending on whether the wife was likely to remarry or whether the children were about to become independent, and taking into account the tax implications of different arrangements for the former partners. Orders for children tended to be made for small amounts and were (and still are) rarely paid regularly or in full. Enforcement procedures were ineffective. Arrangements for separating cohabitants are less well documented but were even less supportive to any resident parent and children. There was no protection for a separated mother who wished to stay in the family home, and child affiliation orders were minimal. The Children Act had made some provision for the resources of couples to be used to benefit their children until those children became economically independent; but these provisions were little known and little used by the cohabiting population.[5] For parents who had never shared a home, the legal remedies were even more perfunctory.

There was little conception at this time of a child's independent right to support from an absent parent. But during the 1980s interest in children as capable individuals with rights grew.[6] At the same time, research was beginning to show that in battles between parents at divorce the interests of children were being overlooked. The issue of child support began to be discussed more widely, particularly as the increase in one-parent families and their dependence on welfare support began to be documented. The divorce and separation epidemic of the 1970s, as well

[4] J Eekelaar and M Maclean, *Maintenance after Divorce* (Oxford, Oxford University Press, 1986).

[5] S Arthur, J Lewis, R Fitzgerald, M Maclean and S Finch, 'Settling Up: Making Financial Arrangements after Separation and Divorce', National Centre for Social Research, 2000.

[6] J Eekelaar, 'Families and Children: From Welfarism to Rights' in JC McCrudden and G Chambers (eds), *Individual Rights and the Law in Britain* (Oxford, Oxford University Press, 1994).

as the growth in the number of children born to parents who had never lived together meant that, by 1987, 14 per cent of all families with children were headed by one parent, and two thirds of them were dependent on the state.[7]

Finally, in 1990 in the case of *Delaney v Delaney*, a father with a second family successfully argued that he should not be required to increase his payments to his first family, as he needed to be able to give his second family a good start in life.[8] The court for the first time accepted the argument that the availability of benefits to the first family was a sufficient reason for the support obligation of an absent parent with a second family to be reduced.

The Development of the Child Support Act

Prime Minister Thatcher responded swiftly to this decision by announcing a policy initiative to 'look at ways of strengthening the system for tracing an absent father and making the arrangements for recovering maintenance more effective'.[9] This Prime Ministerial intervention was clear and insistent. (The term 'hand-bagging' was used behind the scenes to indicate Thatcher's determination on this matter, a reference to both her strength of will and fondness for capacious handbags.) The previous Minister responsible for social security, Norman Fowler, who had carried out a major review of the social security system, was well aware of the difficulties associated with intervention and had resigned his post in order 'to spend more time with his family' as an alternative to having to attempt to deal with the matter. Prime Minister Thatcher then appointed Tony Newton as Minister for Social Security, and he was subject to a firm imperative to develop policy as quickly as possible on this issue.

It has often been said that the Prime Minister's aim was primarily to reduce public spending, in this area as in other spheres of governmental activity. This Government was conservative in its approach to family obligations, believing in individual initiative and responsibility, and wary of excessive state intervention to support those who might be persuaded to help themselves. But those close to her at the time agree that the Prime Minister's main focus was not on cost-saving but on what she saw as the

[7] J Bradshaw and J Millar, 'Lone Parents in the UK', report to the Department of Social Security, 1991.

[8] *Delaney v Delaney* [1990] 2 FLR 457.

[9] *The Independent*, 18 January 1990.

problem of irresponsible fathers who walk away from their children and must accept their responsibilities particularly if they had gone on to have subsequent children.

She required action. The handbag was wielded.

As with the Children Act the policy direction was clear. But in this case there was no lack of ministerial interest, rather the reverse, and above all strong interest and pressure for swift action from the Prime Minister herself.

The approach to the project from within the civil service initially resembled that of the Children Act project: an Interdepartmental Working Group was set up to consider the matter; and Peter Harris, now responsible for Family Policy at the Lord Chancellor's Department, proceeded, as he had done when working on the Children Act, to call in experts.

Maclean was identified as a potential consultant at a seminar held by the independent think-tank the Family Policy Studies Centre, which was discussing plans for a new Australian child support scheme as part of the review of social security. The Australians were seeking to learn from the recent development of a child support scheme in Wisconsin that was masterminded by Professor Irwin Garfinkel, who had an unusual combination of expertise in both economics and child welfare, and were planning reform. The international academic community were in close touch on these matters and provided a rich source of information and ideas to the UK policy officials. Instead of having to work by contacting embassies to discover how child support was handled in different jurisdictions, the academic consultant for the Child Support Bill could simply call a colleague in the relevant country or fire off a fax for an instant and well-informed response.

The existing position in England and Wales was that decision-making by the courts on support obligations was individually tailored to circumstances, often creatively making best use of a family's resources to set up the best possible package of support for mothers and children. In the United Kingdom the rental housing market is small, and house purchase through mortgage is the most common way of providing a family home. It was extremely difficult for a woman with an interrupted or part-time career to achieve the credit rating that would enable her to obtain a mortgage in her own right; but a man with firmer career structure who had started a mortgage could continue it and even begin another. So an effective solution was sometimes to allow a mother and child to stay in the family home, while the Department for Social Security paid mortgage interest (but not principal) repayments for a mother on benefit, and the father was able to re-enter the housing market, losing little except immediate access to the usually small amount of equity accrued in the family home. The process was lengthy and costly to the individuals concerned, who had to pay legal fees, or costly for the state, when these were paid for those in need from the public purse via the Legal Aid Fund.

Though the British courts were adversarial in structure, a legal culture based on negotiation and settlement had developed, led by the Solicitors Family Law Association. Effective economic packages were being worked out, following the primary aim under the Children Act of maximising the welfare of the children involved, often through keeping them in the family home at least in the short term. But in addition to setting up child support arrangements, orders often needed to be taken back to court for enforcement or variation as circumstances changed. The courts lacked the capacity to deal with the volume of work, which led to increasingly lengthy delays, and there were no effective enforcement procedures that could be taken against non-resident parents who failed to pay. The government therefore became increasingly interested in moving away from court-based settlement to the kinds of administrative procedures being developed in other jurisdictions as both cheaper and more helpful.

In the United States a number of state jurisdictions had set out guidelines for the level of child support to be paid after divorce. These were developed from studies of the actual costs of childrearing,[10] which calculated the proportion of income spent on a child or numbers of children by parents and included various modifications to reflect both the needs of an absent parent who might have acquired a second family and the resources of a resident parent who might have acquired extra household resources through the presence of a new partner. The criteria varied but were expressed in formulae requiring payment of a percentage of the liable parent's income. These guidelines were used by the courts, thus simplifying the process of assessing the quantum of child support required when liability was established. The US federal government then set up a child support agency that was tasked with collection and enforcement.

With regard to the scheme in Wisconsin, Garfinkel had articulated a clear principle: even if parents do not share a household with their children, they nonetheless have an obligation to share their resources with their children in the same way they would if sharing a common house-

[10] Eg, Espenshade, T, Investing in Children, (Washington DC,Urban Institute Press, 1984); and Garfinkel, I, 'Child Support Trends in the United States' in L Weitzman and M Maclean (eds), *Economic Consequences of Divorce* (Oxford, Oxford University Press, 1992).

hold. Australian interest in the Wisconsin scheme led to legislation there in 1988–89 that replaced earlier court-based discretionary approaches to child maintenance with a formula determining the amount that a non-custodial parent (NCP) should pay. This was to be assessed, collected and enforced by an administrative agency, the Child Support Agency, with the cooperation of the Inland Revenue Service.[11]

In London the Interdepartmental Working Group included representatives from a wide range of government departments, including the Lord Chancellor's Department (LCD), the Department for Social Security (DSS), the Home Office (HO), Inland Revenue, Treasury and others. As consultant, Maclean, with John Eekelaar, prepared a number of papers on what was happening in other jurisdictions, not only Australia and the US but also some of the more successful Continental European systems that had long experience of using guidelines, such as Switzerland and Austria. We also produced papers raising the question of what exactly the aims of the policy were thought to be and how these were to be prioritised. Was the primary concern to address the issue of child poverty in single-parent households? To reduce the benefit bill? To reduce legal costs and reduce the pressure on the family courts? Or to change ideas amongst the general public about the responsibilities of parents, in line with the philosophy of the Children Act?

A questionnaire was sent round to the government departments involved to seek their views. We suggested that some of these aims could conflict, which made the identification of priorities essential. For example, in requiring resources to be transferred from one household to another to emphasise the obligation of absent parents to the children with whom they no longer shared a home, there was a risk of alleviating poverty in the first family but increasing poverty amongst children of fathers with second families. There was a need to consider which children's welfare was the paramount consideration – those of the first family or those of the second family – especially as rates of marriage breakdown are higher among re-partnered parents with children. Unfortunately, at the time no one had researched public attitudes about how to prioritise these claims in families in which there is simply not sufficient income to sustain both families at a reasonable standard of living.

We also raised questions about the feasibility and desirability of taking such a matter out of the jurisdiction of the courts and placing it in the hands of an administrative agency that could not offer the degree of

[11] For a full account, see N Wikeley, *Child Support: Law and Policy* (Oxford, Hart Publishing, 2006) ch 5.

individual scrutiny and rights of appeal that made the courts an attractive option, despite their functional problems of cost and delay. We asked about the underlying philosophy behind the policy: were we in agreement with Garfinkel's formulation of the principle of income-sharing? What kinds of modifications to an assessment would be required to take into account the needs of fathers with second families and the resources of mothers, particularly those with new partners? How was the money to be collected, given that the Inland Revenue Service had declared itself unwilling to attempt the task? The Treasury representatives argued that any attempt to collect small sums of money from a large group of reluctant fathers would result in an operational failure that would have implications for the successful collection of taxes more generally.

All of these points were fully discussed in the Interdepartmental Working Group, though as advisers we had to learn how to support the process by producing short papers with bullet points rather than the lengthy, fully referenced papers that come more naturally to academics.

Prime Ministerial interest drove the project forward at a breath-taking pace. The consultation papers were prepared for the Interdepartmental Working Group during the spring and early summer of 1990. Later that year, without publishing a Green Paper which sets out government's ideas and invites comment, the government published a White Paper, that is, a statement of governmental aims and plans, entitled 'Children First'.[12] The White Paper was swiftly followed by the Bill, which received Royal Assent the following year – a punishing timetable of 18 months from the first policy announcement to legislation. (In contrast, the Children Act 1989 had taken five years.)

Though kick-started by the Prime Minister's announcement, the policy making process had nevertheless begun from first principles, then considered the necessary questions arising , and worked through each in turn. The appropriate questions had been asked about which children were to be included for assessment, including stepchildren, disabled children and age cut-offs set at 16 or 18 or the end of fulltime education. The toughest challenge was presented by the hypothetical and much discussed example of disabled triplets at university. There were issues about establishing liability and paternity in cases of dispute, in which new developments in DNA testing were, though expensive, to be of great help. There were issues about which agency should collect child support; about the level of protected income on which noncustodial parents

[12] DSS ,Children First: The Government's Proposals on the Maintenance of Children (Cm 1264 October 1990) HMSO London

should not be assessed; and about identifying whether any account should be taken of a resident parent's resources earned or unearned within the household. There were also technical legal questions about how the new administrative system should be constituted and how it should relate to any decision-making by the courts and any machinery for appeal. The Bill took a position that was fully in line with the all-embracing approach of the Children Act, by including all children with non-resident parents, not only those whose parents had married and divorced (as had effectively been the case under the court system).

However, very quickly attention in the DSS focused on the need to set and agree a precise formula to be used in assessing the amount of support to be paid. Far more attention was paid to this than to any other aspect of the Bill. Pressure was put on the officials at the LCD to produce an answer. Maclean and Eekelaar, as well as other lawyers at LCD, remained concerned that taking disputes outside a proper forum for adjudication would have implications for the rule of law. Our Central European colleagues shared our concern as they were then emerging from a legalistic system in which the interest of the state was the law, and administrative decision-making was seen as a poor substitute for the work of the courts.

But our concerns were not solely theoretical or philosophical. There was a practical issue about the possibility of enforcing unpopular administrative decisions that were made without the detailed scrutiny of the courts if those decisions ran counter to the beliefs and expectation of those being asked to pay. A legal system that is forced to carry a law which cannot be enforced is under threat. For this reason, Eekelaar and Maclean proposed, as a first step, moving gradually away from the court-based system towards a basic child support system, with the support obligations to be set at levels with which no one could reasonably raise an objection, even when individual circumstances were not rigorously investigated. We suggested that all non-resident parents should be required to pay a basic payment set at or around the current level of child benefit, the longstanding universal payment from the state to all parents of around £10 per week. This would in effect cover the possible payment that might be reasonably expected from a man with average or below-average earnings and the demands of a second family, without causing hostility and without endangering the operation of the scheme. The great majority of cases were known to involve families with below-average earnings. For the perhaps 10 per cent of cases in which there were more resources available, the courts should continue to make individual assessments and orders.

By this stage, the Prime Minister's original aim of alerting fathers to their responsibilities had received further scrutiny from the Treasury. They argued that the current low tax threshold, combined with the fact that taxpayers were supporting children in one-parent families through the welfare system, meant that in effect poor families containing two adults were subsidising poor families containing one adult. They decided that the right thing to do was therefore to maximise the 'take' from non-resident parents to relieve the pressure of welfare payments on the public purse. Treasury economists decided that the highest percentage of income that could be required from a non-resident parent without removing his incentive to remain in the labour market was 50 per cent, and this should therefore be the top level at which the formula requirement should be set. In the Interdepartmental Working Group the Treasury voice was strong and rarely disputed.[13]

The struggle to set the formula dominated the interdepartmental Whitehall discussions, with DSS demanding that LCD should produce the formula immediately. LCD was in pole position as the department passing a function over to the DSS by removing the matter from courts. But at this stage LCD deliberations were dominated by questions of principle and concerns about access to justice. DSS became impatient with these abstract concerns and wanted to begin calculations of the possible payments that could be expected. As the work proceeded towards the Bill, the gap between the approach of the two key departments widened and, cooperation was not enhanced.

DSS, in keeping with their area of responsibility and experience, approached the matter like the legislative preparation of any other new form of welfare benefit. In this model, an individual claims money from the state and is assessed according to criteria for eligibility. The state, usually with some element of discretion, then decides whether to believe him and whether the benefit is due. Unfortunately, the work of family law is family dispute. The matter of child support reflects a conflict between parents; otherwise they would not be involving any public body, whether courts or welfare authorities. DSS could not understand that in a party–party dispute in which the father says he cannot pay because he has lost his job, and the mother responds that he is working in the black labour market, these allegations need to be investigated; and any information given by one side must be put before the other and tested before a decision can be made. This takes time and resources.

[13] In contrast, during the making of the Children Act 1989, officials had managed to convince Government that there would be no extra costs. Therefore there had been no Treasury involvement in the policy development or drafting. See above chapter 2.

The differences in departmental approach also affected the development of the formula. There were strong arguments for the kind of simplicity and verifiability that underpinned the Australian system, which set percentages of income for the non-resident parents obligation and then worked with the Inland Revenue Service to use an indisputable figure for determining non-resident parent (NRP) income (ie, the previous year's taxable income). Sadly, the United Kingdom had no equivalent figures and had to rely on self-reporting of income, even for those with employers who might have been asked to verify payments.

Furthermore, in an attempt to replicate the detail of the case-sensitive court-based decisions, the formula became increasingly complex, making allowances for the expenditures of non-resident parents by adding their actual housing costs into the formula. These circumstances are of course subject to some alteration, particularly in the period immediately following a divorce or separation, and are extremely hard to verify. In addition, it was suggested that including actual housing costs would give a hostile parent every incentive to maximise his costs to the detriment of the children.

Even though the policy aims in the child support project were reasonably clear and not without merit, they were not easily capable of being incorporated clearly when drafting legislation. The Bill itself remained a skeleton, with much of the detail being incorporated into subsequent lengthy and complex regulations.

The Content of the Child Support Bill

The formula set out the support obligation of non-resident parents as a percentage of assessable income to be required for one, two, three or more children. Assessable income was defined as the income remaining after allowances had been made for the personal needs of a NRP, the needs of any biological children in the NRP's home, and a correction to prevent the NRP household as a whole falling below the minimum income set for income support eligibility. The rate of take was to be 50 per cent until the payor had met as much as he could of the support obligation. Opt-out clauses operated for disabled children or when resources exceeded a certain level. The amount of the support obligation was derived from the amount that the state would have to pay to the children of the first family if they were on benefit. This decision was attractive to officials as these benefit levels were considered to have legitimacy – they are agreed as a minimum living requirement in Parliament and are regularly updated.

These criteria were developed in lengthy meetings that often went late into the evening over a long, hot summer; and achieved a considerable degree of intellectual coherence. However, the concepts were not easy to communicate to the public. The calculation, for example, included an allowance, since reduced, for a parent with care in order to recognise that there are indirect as well as direct costs associated with raising children and that resident parents must either forgo paid work to provide care or pay the cost of child care in order to be able to work. This was clearly marked out as part of childcare costs, not as spousal support payments, but it was not always seen in that light by potential payors.

The resources of new partners were not taken into account on either side of the equation, except when operating the safety net for the paying parent in refraining from driving the second household below the poverty line and onto benefit. The obligation was a direct one between children and biological parents (a point that led later to problems in deciding who could take enforcement action for non-payment, lone parents being unable to do so according to the House of Lords judgment in *Kehoe*).[14]

With the minor exceptions described above, child support ceased to be a matter for the courts. Disputes other than paternity were to be handled by child support tribunals. The arrival of DNA testing made these questions more manageable.

Passage of the Act

In terms of drafting, the Child Support Act differed markedly from the Children Act. There were over 300 pages of initial instructions from the DSS to Parliamentary Counsel, with only two months before the draft Bill was to be put before Parliament. Parliamentary Counsel described to the second Oxford Seminar how the work was completed within three months, at the cost of many late-night sessions. In his words, the legislation did not set out the detail but rather the pegs on which the detail had to be hung. Particular problems arose with the special cases for exemption on which there was minimal policy guidance, and it was hard for

[14] *R (Kehoe) v Secretary of State for Work and Pensions* [2004] EWCA Civ 225; [2004] 1 QB 1378; [2005] UKHL 48.

counsel to work out what was the desired result. The timetable as set out by the Prime Minster left little room for manoeuvre.

The passage of the Bill through its Parliamentary stages was, perhaps surprisingly, relatively smooth. There were well-informed and critical debates in the House of Lords about some of the more draconian aspects of the Bill. For example, the first draft of the Bill enabled child support officers to enter any premises where a non-resident parent might be thought to be earning money and question anyone present about the matter. When Lord McGregor and Lord Mishcon pointed out that this might include questioning by a child support officer of a three-year-old daughter of an architect working at home, the clause was amended. Similarly, the attempt to require a lone parent seeking benefit to identify the father of the child was also amended to a request rather than a requirement. Behind the scenes, DSS agreed to take a soft approach to implementation on this aspect, in view of the concerns of women's groups about mothers who might be victims of domestic violence or abuse.

In the House of Commons there was no serious challenge to the Bill. The standard number of committee hearings were held, and there was no need for more. There was press coverage, but it did not stimulate further debate. The officials were ready with defensive arguments to respond to challenges, which never came. There was quite simply broad cross-party support for the idea that the current system was not working well; tackling the issue was a popular venture. The opposition Labour party had been pressing for action for some time, and so they too had little ground for criticism.

The public debate was superficial. When the Bill was in preparation the press had focused on trying to get prior information about what exactly the formula would contain. Maclean remembers almost falling for the old media trick of a reporter pretending to have knowledge of the details and simply wanting to discuss the implications. There was little public or media interest in the issues of access to a proper forum for decision-making in a dispute, or in the technicalities of impact of the lack of welfare disregards. Some lone parent groups were supportive of the idea of reform, particularly of the idea of helping lone parents to get out of the 'poverty trap'. Under the existing system it was hard for a single mother with childcare problems and without qualifications to earn enough to make coming off benefits and entering the labour market worthwhile. Even a small but regular child maintenance payment would be 'portable' income, which would stay with her as she entered the labour market, unlike the welfare benefits, which stopped when earnings began.

Others were becoming aware of the possibility that the current demand-led legal aid fund might soon be capped, in which case human rights issues were likely to ensure that criminal legal aid would take the lion's share, as those in danger of losing their liberty had a right to proper advice and representation. If the level of funds were to become fixed, there would be little remaining for family legal aid, on which many women relied when seeking spousal or child support orders and enforcement. In these circumstances, an administrative entitlement began to look more attractive than a legal claim.

But there were concerns. Some thought the measure draconian in the demands to access information about individual circumstances – personal as well as financial. The legislation empowered officials to enquire into the paternity of children in a non-resident parent's household, as well as his earnings; and it gave no leeway to those seeking to make more complex arrangements through the courts whereby regular transfer payments from the NRP might be traded by the parent with care for a larger share of the property, particularly the family home. Others objected to the government's insistence on having no welfare disregard, ie, taking into account every pound of child support when assessing the household for benefit entitlement.

The Bill came with a double-layer framework, not only general regulations but also Section 42, which gave blanket powers to define special circumstances. The aim was to provide flexibility in areas where things were likely to go wrong.

It may be that the Prime Minister's pressure to keep to time in moving this legislation forward was caused by the expectation of a general election in the autumn of 1990. But instead of an election, Thatcher was succeeded by John Major, leading a Conservative but less confident administration. In the event, the new Prime Minister had other matters of more immediate concern and took little interest in the child support legislation, with the result that the timetable rolled on undisturbed. One result of the rapid timetable was that by the time the original consultation period ended, there was already a first draft of the Bill. There was a good deal of response from over 150 consultees, from a wide range of organisations, and some detailed points were changed to reflect their suggestions. But as the responses were to a White Paper rather than a Green Paper, it was not unusual for the general shape of the legislation to have been pre-decided.

A longer consultation period would have given more time to get back to grassroots and discover what was going on in practice. But the general idea of a service for parents remained widely supported. It was only after the consultation period ended that alarm bells began to ring. There was no unwillingness by officials to listen to ideas, only a shortage of time in which to do so. There was also the difficulty that some groups were entirely opposed to the reform because they believed that families should be supported by the state; that matters should not be removed from courts; or that maintenance should not be considered separately from access. These groups had little in common and failed to present any serious or united opposition to the Bill.

Looking Back at the Child Support Act

As we suggested above, at first sight this legislative project appears to have had much in common with the Children Act 1989. In both cases the making of a law responded to an issue of widespread concern; there was consensus about the need for action. In the case of the Child Support Bill, as with the Children Act, ideas were extensively canvassed from other jurisdictions, and research findings were commissioned and carefully studied. As with the Children Act, there was a general debate about the division of responsibility between the state and individuals for the care and protection of children.

Before the Children Act there had been public debate about how proactive the state should be in intervening in family life in order to protect children at risk of abuse or neglect, and a line was carefully drawn which required a court to find evidence of risk before action would be taken. In the case of the Child Support Bill there was public debate about whether the state or individuals should take responsibility for the financial support of children in a society that widely accepted serial adult partnerships. In both cases there was little concerted opposition to the Bills, and they did not become the subject of party political concern. Neither was heavily amended in its passage through Parliament. The philosophy of the Child Support Act was consistent with that of the Children Act, putting child welfare first and attempting to codify a practical response to children at risk – in this case, of poverty due to parental absence. In addition, the Child Support Act, like the Children Act, accepted responsibility for all children, not only those of divorcing parents, as had been the case previously.

So why did the Child Support Act give rise almost immediately to universal criticism and become subject to almost immediate revision and subsequent repeal? There were serious issues associated with implementation. The system could have been implemented quite simply, but the decision was taken to put some hundred variables into the equation for calculating payment due. There was little understanding of the lack of stability in these parent's lives, with rapidly changing employment, housing and personal circumstances. The much criticised recent tax credit system is a more recent victim of the problems of verification that this gives rise to.

There was also little understanding of the fact that child support is a matter of dispute between parents, which is problematic for an administrative system that requires ticks in boxes and lacks the flexibility and discretion exercised by the courts. The Agency itself was set up with insufficient resources, and with staff who lacked the necessary qualifications and experience. Senior management lacked a degree of sensitivity and flexibility. Furthermore, the expectations of what the new dedicated computer system would be able to offer were wildly optimistic. The enterprise was seriously hampered by information technology and computing problems, a common enough story across Whitehall that has changed little over the past 20 years.

The legislation also provided for the new Child Support Agency to be established outside government as a Next Steps Agency, as part of the Conservative government's attempts to reduce the scale of government and encourage more forms of independent enterprise in public service. But rather than offering the freedom associated with private enterprise, this structure in fact contributed to rigidity of management and a lack of transparency and accountability in the early stages. Finally, the Agency was overwhelmed by its workload, unable to prioritise benefit cases when the circumstances of each case were volatile and hard to establish, when there was little money to be had from non-resident parents, and when there was no incentive for mothers with care of children to cooperate, as they received no financial advantage in the absence of a welfare disregard.

All these factors, particularly the speed with which Prime Minister Thatcher drove the matter forward, made the process of innovation difficult. But perhaps the root cause of the unpopularity was the nature of the task that the Act was trying to accomplish. Instead of a fair but overburdened court system that took pains to investigate individual circumstances, made finely-tuned decisions and then often failed to implement them, we had the introduction of a universal but rigid system that lacked the discretion traditionally exercised by both courts and benefit systems; it demanded money from all non-resident parents and seemed to do so while using inaccurate information and without sensitivity to the position of either parent. The government's argument was that all this was being done to benefit the children concerned. However, it rapidly became widely believed that the chief beneficiary, with the connivance of the government, was to be the Treasury. The Child Support Act demanded increased amounts (typically £40 per week rather than £20) from men who were not only unwilling to pay but often had real problems in supporting the present family with whom they had now chosen to live rather the former family where problems had arisen. The mothers, 80 per cent of whom had spent some time as welfare recipients, had not only no financial incentive to seek the help of the Child Support Agency but a strong disincentive to do so, as it might damage the already fragile on-going relationships with the fathers of their children.

Was this simply a case of a law-making exercise that was too driven from above? Was there simply insufficient time for discussion and consensus-building, for identifying the practical difficulties through consultation with those on the ground and for commissioning the in-depth research that would have told us about the circumstances of these families? Were the problems exacerbated by the insistence of the Treasury on the maximum rate of take, by the lack of understanding between the DSS and LCD about the nature of the agency being created and by the lack of proper resources to do the work required? Or, given the problems subsequently encountered in the United States and Australia, is this simply an area that legislation simply cannot solve? In other words, is the financial problem of two families depending on one major breadwinner beyond the scope of legislation alone? If society accepts serial partnering, should it bite the bullet and pay for the children out of public funds?

The contrast between the Children Act and the Child Support Act helps us to raise more fundamental questions about what constitutes a successful law-making project. If a statute is clearly drafted and does not need to be elaborated or tested in the courts, the drafting lawyers generally count it as successful. If the implementation is smooth and the statute has a long life, officials are content. Their political masters will ask for immediate popularity and potential votes – and without additional costs – which might be construed as adherence to the Benthamite utilitarian values of the greater happiness of the greatest number.

But there may be other criteria for success, and the difference in outcome between these two legislative enterprises may not be as great as it appears. There is no case for denigrating the Children Act, an entirely successful piece of legislation, which went beyond technical codification to philosophical reconciliation in its approach to child welfare and has since been imitated in jurisdictions from Australia to Bulgaria. But we may wish to reconsider the impact of the Child Support Act. We may wish to raise two long-term cheers for the Child Support Act, despite all the problems described. It seems with hindsight that the Child Support Act may have achieved Prime Minster Thatcher's aim of raising awareness about the need for non-resident fathers to accept financial responsibility for their children. The views of the public about who should be supporting which children have changed in the 15 years since the Act was passed. Most of those directly affected by the Child Support Act, especially non-resident parents, do not like the orders that are made in their own specific cases. But notwithstanding this, there is now new and widespread acceptance that parents, rather than leaving the matter entirely to the state, have an obligation to support their children, regardless of their relationship with the other parent and regardless of their own circumstances or those of the other parent.

The unpopularity of the legislation and the agency it created may in the future transform into grudging recognition that the short term pain of the payors has had long-term benefits for the children of separated parents. That said, recent reforms to make the process simpler, with a less complex formula and a clearer definition of income to be assessed, together with the possibility of a welfare disregard, have been long overdue. The Child Maintenance and Other Payments Act 2008 established the Child Maintenance and Enforcement Commission as a non-departmental public body. These legislative reforms gambled on the new level of public acceptance of responsibility for financial support for children by encouraging a return to private parental support arrangements and moving away from the universal state intervention of the Child Support Act 1991. The indications of success are fragile so far. The information placed in the House of Commons Library on 12 July 2010 in response to a Parliamentary question on levels of arrears by Parliamentary constituency is not encouraging.[15] But if progress is beginning to be made, and if this proves to be either substantial or durable, the Child Support Act 1991 may yet find itself alongside the Children Act as a successful legislative project and an effective element in the fundamental programme of family law-making in England and Wales.

[15] See above n 2.

4

Campaigns and Tactics: Batman & Robin and the Children and Adoption Act 2006

WE BEGAN THIS volume with a reminder of the caveats about the difficulty of reforming family law and the complexity of the often contentious policy issues. These matters are hard to reflect in clear legal drafting, and harder still to implement effectively, as they usually require troubled and conflicted individuals to behave in a rational and altruistic manner: a tall order. As Ira Ellman put it in his inaugural lecture, 'Making family law is hard'.[1]

After examining the apparently the successful codification of child law in the Children Act 1989, as well as the troubled though perhaps eventually surprisingly effective attempt by the then Prime Minister to impose a financial obligation on absent parents in the Child Support Act 1991, we turn now to a rather different law-making project. Rather than responding to a widespread, broadly based concern in society about child protection or child support, the government, in the case of the Children and Adoption Act 2006, was forced to react tactically to the activities of a particular group of unsatisfied customers of the family justice system. In the late 1990s a number of fathers' rights groups emerged, representing the views of non-resident parents who wish to have more time with their children after separation or divorce. Given changing social attitudes towards the involvement of both parents with their children and a more equal balance between work in the home and paid work outside, and in the context of the development of family policy based on supporting parents by the Labour administration,[2] this might appear to be a movement that government should be more than willing to support.

[1] Ellman, I, 'Why Making Family Law is Hard' (2003) 35(3) *Arizona State Law Journal* 699.

[2] Home Office, 'Supporting Families: A Consultation Document' (London, HMSO, 1998).

But family law is rarely that simple. Although the fathers' movement spanned a wide area of interest and competence, with many groups helpfully providing practical advice (such as recipes and games for children under five years of age), this particular campaign was spearheaded by one of the most extraordinary activist groups seen in the United Kingdom for many years. Fathers for Justice or 'F4J' were highly visible. Their leaders, often dressed as Batman and Robin, carried out daring exploits to publicise their cause: they successfully scaled Buckingham Palace and the House of Commons; and they handcuffed Margaret Hodge, then Minister for Children, at a Law Society Conference in Manchester in November 2003. They finally disbanded in some disarray after an undercover television documentary revealed their support for physical attacks on ex-wives and a failed plan to abduct the youngest child of Prime Minister Tony Blair.

Maclean was present at the handcuffing incident and can confirm the aggression that was displayed and the distress caused by this assault, none of which was ever punished through a court of law. In the early stages in 2002–04, the campaign was successful in attracting support from a wide section of the media, including mainstream newspapers and television programmes. The fathers' groups presented the courts as biased towards women, unwilling or unable to make appropriate orders concerning contact between non-resident parents and their children, and unable to enforce such orders when a resident parent was not compliant.

England and Wales were not alone in experiencing these protests, though the issue never gained a high profile in Scotland. In 1999 in Paris the first international conference on the work of contact centres in supporting the relationships between absent fathers and their children was besieged by angry fathers. Similar demonstrations followed in Canada and in Australia, where groups of extremist fathers in black clothing and masks kept overnight vigil outside the homes of single mothers thought to be limiting paternal access to their children. These were extreme measures, but similar events followed in England, where the F4J claimed to be modelling its direct action tactics on those of the women suffragettes seeking the vote before the First World War, and they even adopted the suffragette colours of green and purple.

These protesters believed that they were being denied the opportunity to play a meaningful part in the lives of their children after separation or divorce by their ex-partners, and they felt that they were unable to find justice as a result of the connivance or ineffectuality of the courts. They demanded a change in the law to give them 'shared parenting', by which the more extreme groups meant the right to half of their children's time.

An average timetable for access arrangements for a non-resident parent at that time would usually have included one evening a week, every other weekend and extended time during school holidays.

What does a democratic government do when faced with such a public outcry, especially when it has gathered widespread public support? Given that the media had initially been sympathetic, and media response means voter impact, which is immediately reported by the pollsters, no government could afford to ignore such claims, especially in England and Wales, where a general election was in prospect.

Background

There were a number of factors behind the demands of fathers' groups. There were clearly some disturbed individuals involved. A recent study by the New Zealand Court Service had made a retrospective analysis of the contact cases before the New Zealand Family Courts in which conflict had become entrenched and found that untreated mental illness was overrepresented among this group of the population.[3] The fathers involved were also less likely to be legally represented and thus often expressed demands that were unconstrained by lawyers as intermediaries, who could draw on legal expertise and experience.[4]

However, there was also a more general movement towards a changing work–life balance, with fathers spending a little more time with their children (though studies showed that the 'new man's time with his children was often restricted to recreational activities) and women spending a little more time in paid work (though this work was often part-time and poorly paid). A third factor in England was the impact of a rapidly developing rights discourse, stimulated by the Human Rights Act 1998, with its protection of privacy and family life.

During this period the media paid increasing attention to fathers' rights, despite the focus of the Children Act 1989 on parental responsibilities, and showed less concern for the welfare of children, which was the paramount consideration enshrined in the Children Act. In addition, connections were made with the Child Support legislation, which, according to activist fathers, required them to pay for children who they

[3] H Barwick, A Gray and R Macky, 'Characteristics Associated with Early Identification of Complex Family Court Cases' (Wellington, New Zealand Department of Courts, 2003).
[4] Ibid.

were not allowed to see. Although the legal framework still maintains a strict division between the obligation of a father to provide financial support and the need for everyone to consider the best interests of the child in reaching any decision about conflicted contact, nevertheless the link is often made.

In the face of fathers' demands for reform of the law relating to child contact in England, what did the government do? The then Prime Minister Blair needed to deal with vociferous criticism of the family justice system. While wanting this 'media noise' to stop, he appeared willing, at least initially, to consider going some way towards meeting these media-worthy demands. This view was intimated to the Department responsible for family law, the Lord Chancellor's Department (now retitled the Department for Constitutional Affairs (DCA)). The departmental Ministers responsible took the Prime Minister's views but were gradually influenced by the advice of officials, who had been informed by expert advice and research evidence, not to move precipitously in the direction requested by the fathers without great care and full consideration of the risks to the children involved.

The role played by research in this particular legislative process was a surprisingly powerful one. The relationship between research and policy formation is always complex. In the late 1960s, students of social policy at the London School of Economics were taught that there are two possible modes for positive interaction between research and policy: a government might value research that endorses decisions which have already been taken; a government might also appreciate the usefulness of lengthy and detailed research when wishing to delay decision-making. But in the case of the contact debate discussed here, a third mode can be identified: research findings acted as a sandbag, ie, the bags that citizens fill with sand and use to defend their homes against flooding. In facing the demands of F4J, the government, which was committed to evidence-based policy-making, needed a defence against the tide of anecdotal and sometimes ill-informed popular pressure to meet the fathers' demands. They sought and found a more objective policy position based on scientific research evidence.

The single-issue media campaign run by the extremist fathers' pressure groups relied on sweeping generalisations and on individual anecdote. Celebrities came to support the cause, notably Sir Bob Geldof, who significantly raised the profile of the issue. The Minister responsible for this policy area within the DCA (formerly LCD), Lord Filkin, was interested in research findings but was also open to discussion with a broad range of stakeholders. He gave radio interviews that were interpreted as showing sympathy for the fathers' position. Sir Bob was a frequent and visible visitor to the Department and, using colourful language, made known his highly critical views of the family courts following his own case, which concerned his high-profile divorce from Paula Yates and the custody of their two daughters. He had eventually on appeal gained residence of all three children, including his stepdaughter following the death of his former wife, but had found the court experience very difficult. He published his thoughts in a chapter entitled 'The Real Love that Dare Not Speak its Name' in a collection of academic essays in 2003.[5] The openness of the Minister to external discussion was admirable and informative; but by being so unusually accessible in some cases, he gave the impression to those who took part that their personal views were being heard with sympathy, and this tended to have the unfortunate effect of increasing their dissatisfaction when their advice was not followed.

As the groundswell of public debate increased, the Prime Minister required action. The DCA had already carried out a programme of work described as Consumer Strategy to try to discover through desk research and some empirical work how the public viewed the courts service and to consider how improvements might be made as the unified courts service was set up, bringing magistrates and county courts together. Building on this work, a strategic approach to family policy was being developed.

The DCA also had a Research Secretariat, which had been commissioning empirical work on contact for some years, notably from the universities of East Anglia and Leeds. Reports by Professors Liz Trinder, Carol Smart and their colleagues into the kinds of cases that were coming to the courts and the way in which some were being helped by the new In-Court Conciliation schemes whereby conflicted parents were helped to negotiate at the door of the court made a significant contribution to the understanding of the nature of contact disputes.[6] Maclean, as Academic Adviser to the Department and Director of the Oxford Centre for Family Law and Policy, was well placed not only to feed into the policy discussions relevant research from the United Kingdom but to draw on international contacts (now by email rather than phone and fax, as it had been in the days of the Child Support project).

[5] Geldof, B, 'The Real Love that Dare Not Speak its Name' in A Bainham, B Lindley, M Richards and E Trinder (eds), *Children and Their Families: Contact, Rights and Welfare* (Oxford, Hart Publishing, 2003).

[6] See L Trinder, J Connolly, J Kelect, C Notley and L Swift, 'Making Contact Happen or Making Contact Work?', Department for Constitutional Affairs (DCA) Research Series 3/06, 2006; C Smart, V May, A Wade and C Furniss, *Residence and Contact Disputes in Court: Volume 1*, DCA Research Series 6/03, 2003; and C Smart et al, *Residence and Contact Disputes in Court: Volume 2*, DCA Research Series 4/05, 2005.

Extensive programmes of empirical work were underway in Canada and Australia, and those findings were particularly helpful when the parallel developments in those jurisdictions were in danger of being misunderstood by Ministers and officials in the United Kingdom. For example, Bob Geldof was widely quoted in the press as saying that Denmark had recently changed its family law to give parents equal time with their children. This remark gained wide coverage but was without any factual base, and it was largely due to the academic connections of the Research Secretariat that a proper understanding of the position in Denmark could be eventually arrived at.

After departmental ministers on the Prime Minister's instructions began to consider the matter, officials in both the DCA and the Department for Education and Skills (DfES), which had recently taken responsibility for bringing all services for children together, began to work on the issues. As policy work on the topic began to develop, Maclean was asked to organise briefings on the existing state of knowledge on child contact for Ministers from the relevant departments: the DCA, the DfES, the Department of Social Security, the Solicitor General, the Department for Work and Pensions (because of their interest in child support) and the Department for Trade and Industry (which housed the gender equality unit). Further detailed briefings were held with Charles Clark, then Secretary of State for Education, and his departmental ministers, including Margaret Hodge, the Minister for Children, who was subsequently physically attacked by F4J (see above).

These sessions included brief and powerful presentations by the key researchers in the field, who then made themselves fully available to the DCA for further consultation during the course of the developing child contact project. In particular, extensive use was made of the Family Policy Briefing Papers funded by the Nuffield Foundation and produced in Oxford by Joan Hunt with Ceridwen Roberts, formerly of the Family Policy Studies Centre.[7] Roberts had developed the fine art of putting key items of research information into clearly presented eight-page documents for MPs and other interested non-specialists. These papers were cleverly produced with bright red covers, so that they remain highly visible amidst the traditional flurry of papers that inevitably appears as a bill approaches Parliament and briefings multiply. All the research

[7] J Hunt and C Roberts, 'Child Contact with Non-resident Parents', Family Policy Briefing Paper 3 (University of Oxford Department of Social Policy and Social Work, 2004); and J Hunt and C Roberts, 'Intervening in Litigated Contact: Ideas from Other Jurisdictions', Family Policy Briefing Paper 4 (University of Oxford Department of Social Policy and Social Work, 2005).

included is fully referenced and summarised, and the papers were handed out generously, thanks to the Nuffield Foundation.

The briefing papers provided a sound evidence base for the DCA and DfES project teams, who needed at this early stage to consider the following key questions:

1. Is contact with an absent parent beneficial to children?
2. Who are the parents who cannot resolve their difficulties over contact after separation?
3. What is the nature of these parental disputes?

The research evidence on Question 1 was at first sight contradictory, with one major study showing unequivocally that more contact is associated with fewer adjustment problems for children[8] and another showing no effect and instead emphasising the effects that the quality of the relationships in a resident household has on a child's development and well-being.[9] The most useful overview was the report of international research by Pryor and Rodgers, which showed that it is the nature and quality of contact that is crucial, not the amount.[10] They argue that the mere presence of fathers is not enough. To the extent that men remain involved in parenting after divorce or assume parenting practices that they have not done before, they have a positive influence. As in intact families, the most effective way they can parent is by providing authoritative parenting, and it is these aspects of parenting encompassing monitoring, encouragement, love and warmth that are consistently linked with well-being.

This useful and dispassionate review contains no easy message that can be succinctly translated into policy terms, especially when the policymakers are facing demands from men who believe they can provide this kind of benefit to their children and from women who do not share this view. Marjorie Smith's finding that the quality of relationships in a child's home is the strongest predictor of health and welfare is a particularly difficult message for angry fathers to hear.[11]

If we go on to the second question about parents, the data showed strongly how few parents (less than 10 per cent of separating parents) have difficulties that they cannot resolve other than by seeking the help of lawyers and courts. And of these, only a small minority fail to reach

[8] J Dunn 'Contact and Children's Perspectives on Parental Relationships' in A Bainham, B Lindley, M Richards and L Trinder (eds) *Children and their Families: Contact Rights and Welfare* (Oxford,Hart Publishing, 2003).

[9] Smith M Robertson, J Dixon, M Quigley and E Whitehead 'A Study of Stepchildren and Stepparenting' report to the Department of Health (2001).

[10] J Pryor and B Rodgers, *Children in Changing Families* (Oxford, Blackwell, 2001).

[11] See above n 9.

agreement and proceed to adjudication. The Office for National Statistics survey for the DCA had found that those who returned to court more than once were not necessarily embroiled in conflict, but rather the majority did so either to clarify an order or to vary the order in response to changed circumstances. (For example, a move by one parent to another town might require more overnight contact; or a child simply becoming older might mean that he or she wishes to spend more time with friends of his or her own age, and reduced contact hours might therefore be sought.)

In response to the third question about the nature of the disputes, the research commissioned by the DCA from Liz Trinder showed that mothers and fathers tend to have different kinds of issues.[12] Non-resident fathers feel excluded from their children's lives and seek to re-establish some control over the situation. Mothers tend to be more focused on welfare issues and lack confidence in fathers' abilities to cope with the practical side of childcare – food, warmth and safety – particularly if there are problems of alcohol or substance abuse by a father or a new partner.

In addition, throughout the research ran a constant thread of references to violence and abuse. Although most children enjoy contact and many of the children studied wanted more than they had, there were children who were distressed by it, sometimes because of harassment or abuse; because parents failed to turn up as promised; because they felt the pressure of divided loyalties; or because they were exposed to parental conflict. Some children reported being used as a go-between in their parents' relationship; of having difficult relationships with their parents' new partners; missing the resident parent when away from home on visits to the non-resident parent. Some simply described the stress of continually moving between two homes, not only because of simple things like remembering their spare shoes or school assignments but also because of the more complicated pressure of adjusting to different lifestyles, in particular, different parenting styles and expectations.[13]

These research findings were up to date, clearly expressed, well founded and accessible to the policy team. Nevertheless, as a body of work the research was problematic because the messages were complex and did not sit easily with the demands of the fathers' groups; nor did

[12] Trinder et al (above n 6).

[13] See A O' Quigley 'Listening to Children's Views: The Findings and Recommendations of Recent Research' (Joseph Rowntree Foundation, 1999); J Hunt, *Researching Contact* (London, National Council for One Parent Families, 2003); Smart et al (2003) (above n 6); and Smart et al (2005) (above n 6).

they make it easy to reject the demands. If contact is good when it it good and bad when it is bad, who is to decide what is good and what is bad? The mother, the father, the child, the professionals . . . or, ultimately, the court?

By this stage, work on the response to the fathers had become a joint project with the DfES, which had taken responsibility for all work with children except that directly undertaken by the courts. The DfES had also taken over responsibility for the troubled former Family Court Welfare Service, now the Children and Family Court Advisory and Support Service (CAFCASS). Cooperation between the two departments was close and productive, eased by the fact that a number of officials had moved from one department to the other as part of the change in responsibilities and were therefore familiar with both the policy and the way of working in the other department. Some were former colleagues and knew each other well (as had been the case in the lead-up to Children Act 1989).

Canada and Australia had by this time responded to their men's pressure groups by holding independent inquiries. In these countries the research evidence led the inquiries, both of which had started from a position that was favourable to the fathers' demands and then moved to a more child-focused approach. The Canadian report, citing the Canadian Charter of Rights and Freedoms, upheld the duty to respect the needs of individual children.[14] The Australian report, entitled 'Every Picture Tells a Story', held to the view that there should be no formulaic approach to contact and that each case should be looked at individually; and it stated clearly that decisions should be made for each child based on that child's needs.[15]

The Australian report, however, was considerably modified by the Parliamentary committee responsible for policy in this area, and the result was the Family Law Amendment (Shared Parental Responsibility) Act 2006, which supported shared parenting responsibility and encouraged more equal contact time between parents. Sadly, February 2008 saw the publication in Australia of an evaluation showing that this had been stressful for many children.[16] Further evaluation studies published in

[14] For a full discussion of the Australian and Canadian developments see H Rhoades and SB Boyd 'Reforming Custody Laws: A Comparative Study' (2004) 18 *International Journal of Law, Policy and the Family* 119.

[15] House of Representatives, Standing Committee on Family and Community Affairs, 'Every Picture tells a Story': Report on the Inquiry into Child Custody Arrangements in the Event of Family Separation (Australian Government Publishing Service, 2003).

[16] J McIntosh and C Long, 'The Child-Responsive Program, Operating within the Less Adversarial Trial: A Follow-Up Study of Parent and Child Outcomes', report to the Family Court of Australia, 2007.

2010 have identified problems with domestic violence when shared parenting is imposed by court order. In February 2010 in the *National Times*, Belinda Fehlberg described how fathers had been encouraged to seek shared care and how mothers felt pressured into it; she also reported that it is now being used by a substantial minority of highly conflicted parents with mental health issues and/or substance abuse problems and that it is being agreed to or ordered by the courts in cases when it does not appear to be iin the child's best interests.[17] A more recent report published in 2010 by Jennifer McIntosh and Bruce Smyth also underlines the significant negative impact of shared care arrangements on children under four years of age, regardless of socioeconomic background, parental or inter-parental cooperation.[18] This report concludes that shared care is not of itself better for children in comparison with other care arrangements, and there therefore seems little justification for the current Australian legislative approach. Fehlberg subsequently argued again in the *National Times* for 'laws that require us to determine children's best interests on a case-by-case basis without preconceived ideas, and laws that require us to take family violence seriously at every step along the way'.[19]

In England and Wales, we did not go so far or so fast in the shared parenting direction as the Australians, though the debate is still a live one following the formation of the new Coalition Government in May 2010.

By the beginning of 2004 drafting had begun in the DCA on a Green Paper to be developed jointly by the DCA and DfES. There was ministerial sympathy for the plight of fathers who are unable to have satisfactory relationships with their children as a result of not having enough time together to develop it, and there was some interest in establishing 50/50 shared time as the starting point in contact arrangements. There was also interest in developing contact guidelines for the conciliation services to use in mediation and for courts to use in coming to contact decisions. One way of achieving this was thought to be through the development of 'parenting plans', which could be issued by government and would give examples of different kinds of circumstances, the problems they give rise to and ways of tackling them (eg, for children of different ages and for parents with different levels of conflict). Advice included, for example, the suggestion that when speaking to the other parent on the

[17] B Fehlberg, *National Times*, 3 February 2010.

[18] J McIntosh, B Smyth, M Kelaher, Y Wells and C Long, 'Post-separation Parenting Arrangements and Developmental Outcomes for Infants and Children: Collected Reports', report to the Australian Attorney General's Department, May 2010.

[19] *National Times*, 20 August 2010.

phone about a coming contact visit, the conversation should be kept to the practical details and should not range into past history or current accusations.

This part of the policy work provides a clear example of the shifting sand of policy refinement. There are fine lines between: a policy recommendation for treating every contact case individually; providing conflicted parents with information about the way some issues are resolved in some families; encouraging conciliation services or courts to recommend these ideas; and legislating guidelines for parents to follow, which might become legal presumptions, rebuttable or not in practice.

There was little disagreement within policy circles about the need for help and advice for parents, but at the same time there was little agreement about precisely where the distinctions described above should be drawn. These disagreements on detail where there is good agreement on the broad brush approach are perhaps the hardest kinds of disagreement to work through, as neither side can see why someone who is clearly sensible enough to take the broad central position can be so foolish as to disagree on the detail. But the devil is in the detail. The genuine difficulty of minute-taking notwithstanding, there were times during the legislative process when differences between the assumptions being made by those present at a meeting meant that interpreting the general tenor of the meeting, let alone understanding its outcome, was highly problematic. The frequent visits of external stakeholders to the Ministers made for continuing input of ideas, which while potentially helpful, also tended to muddy the distinctions usually drawn between the different stages of law-making work. These may be characterised as ministerial proposal and request for advice; provision of information and advice by officials; followed by ministerial decision on action, after which policy officials move towards developing a Green paper for consultation, followed by a White paper that sets out the government's plans.[20] By that point it should be possible to draft clear instructions for the departmental lawyer, who will instruct the Parliamentary draftsman responsible for drafting the Bill to be presented to Parliament. New input at this stage is hard to handle, especially as time pressures inevitably build up once Parliamentary time has been allocated.

[20] For the Green Paper and White Paper in the context of the Children and Adoption Act, see Department for Constitutional Affairs, Department for Education and Skills and Department of Trade and Industry, *Parental Separation: Children's Needs and Parents' Responsibilities* (Green Paper, Cm 6273, 2004); and HM Government, *Next Steps: Report of the Responses to Consultation and Agenda for Action* (White Paper, Cm 6452, 2005).

Not only were there continuing new suggestions arising from interested parties outside the departments, but there were also overlapping policy issues within the DCA and DfES that had to be taken into account. For example, within DCA it had been established policy since the mid-1980s that courts were to be seen only as a service of last resort. It was thought better for individuals to avoid the possible aggravation of conflict endemic to our adversarial system and to be encouraged and supported in resolving or managing disputes through alternative methods of dispute resolution. This policy was also seen as helpful with regard to the Legal Aid budget, which needed to be restrained or reduced. Any change with regard to contact arrangements for non-resident parents and children had therefore to be supported by alternative dispute resolution rather than court-based procedures.

A number of procedures based on this principle began to be put forward by stakeholders and to attract the attention of ministers and policy officials. In particular, a programme developed by Judge John Lederman in Florida known as the Early Intervention Project became widely discussed and influenced the Government in agreeing to set up a pilot scheme for early intervention in these conflicted contact cases, known as the Family Resolutions Pilot (FRP). Maclean was invited to chair the Design Board for this project, with a team of representatives from the courts service, the judiciary, the legal profession, policy officials from the DCA and DfES, representatives of the groups working with conflicted parents and representatives of those working in parenting education. We were asked to rapidly prepare a pilot project and were bombarded by advocates of a variety of schemes, and a variety of individual views ranging from those in favour of directing parents towards 50/50 shared-time parenting to maintaining the Children Act position of treating each case on its merits and putting the welfare of the child as the paramount consideration in any decision being made about that child's care and upbringing.

Every member of the FRP pilot design group had the children's interests at heart, but every member held a different view about how this could be achieved. The situation paralleled the situation the programme was trying to address – two parents in deep conflict who are both convinced that only they have the child's best interests at heart and, more importantly, know how to provide for the child. Members of the design group became highly conflicted from time to time only because of their deep conviction that only they had the solution.

Eventually a scheme was piloted that was based on group work with conflicted parents, something that had not been tried before in this jurisdiction. Mothers and fathers, though not from the same couple, were brought together to watch a short film made for the FRP that showed the experience of separation from the child's point of view in a short dramatised scene, followed by an unscripted discussion among young people from a drama school. These were young people who might or might not have experienced parental separation but were confident and articulate in front of the camera. The conflicted parents were then led in discussion at a second meeting by relationship counsellors and parent education specialists, focusing on how parents might best meet their children's needs at this difficult time. In a third and final meeting, parents came together to work on their own parenting plan with a CAFCASS officer.

It was instructive to see how this modest scheme was attacked from various quarters for not replicating the Florida scheme exactly (though there were legal reasons for this); for not being mandatory (again, legally impossible without primary legislation); for not setting out presumptions about preferred parenting arrangements (even though the terms of reference had excluded any prescriptive action that would conflict with the Children Act); and so on. For Maclean it was instructive to see at first hand the difficulty of developing something new as a group, to be put into practice amidst sincerely held but conflicting views – in contrast to the traditional academic role of advising government, which entails making rather grand or general suggestions as an individual or pointing out the actual or potential flaws in any system.

Robust input from the research side continued to emphasise the importance of the quality rather than the amount of parental contact with children, and from the departmental lawyers came strong support for maintaining the paramountcy principle of the Children Act 1989. At the end of the day, the Green Paper was published in July 2004, clearly setting out its position in the title, 'Parental Separation: Children's Needs and Parents' Responsibilities'.[21] There was no discussion of fathers' rights, and there was a robust defence of the child paramountcy principle. The Paper set out the facts of the matter, noting that only 10 per cent of separating parents seek a legal solution to a contact problem, and of these only a very small minority fail to settle and must go to adjudication. The Paper acknowledged that the present system was not working well but firmly rebutted any suggestion of bias against non-resident parents in the family courts and any suggestion that the Children Act should be modified. It focused instead on ways of helping parents to resolve their disputes by out-of-court methods. The Paper was supported by a fully

[21] See ibid.

referenced account of existing research information, posted on the DfES departmental website.

Furthermore, the Paper demonstrated the close cooperation between the newly reconstituted DfES and the DCA. Chapter one began by quoting the DfES Green Paper published in 2003, entitled 'Every Child Matters', which set out five key outcomes that matter for every child: being healthy; staying safe; enjoying and achieving; making a positive contribution; and economic well-being.[22] Paragraph 3 reaffirmed the philosophy of the Children Act, the paramountcy of a child's welfare in any court decision affecting the care of that child, but it further affirmed the need to ascertain and take into account the wishes and feelings of the child depending on the child's age and level of understanding. Paragraph 6 stated that the government believes each parent has a responsibility to ensure their child has meaningful contact with the other parent: a non-resident parent has a responsibility to sustain his or her relationship with the child, while the resident parent has a responsibility to enable this to happen. Both are equally important to the child. It is then acknowledged that any family dispute is unlikely to be resolved through a single intervention; instead, parents will need support and advice as part of a continuing process, and the Paper promises proposals to make this happen.

Although the changing patterns of parenting by mothers and fathers was acknowledged by the 2004 Green Paper, Children's Needs and Parents Responsibilities, and the importance of both parents to children was stressed, the demand of the fathers' groups for a presumption of shared parenting as evidenced by the amount of time spent with each parent had, in effect, been rejected. Fathers of course retained the parental responsibility that they had held since the Children Act 1989. This legislative project remained true to the Children Act ideology and terminology by putting children first and rejecting any formulaic approach to regulating contact (unlike the formulaic approach accepted with such unpopular results in the Child Support Act 1991).

By this stage the fathers' rights groups were beginning to lose media sympathy as F4J exploits became more and more extreme and as the women's groups began to raise concerns about violence and abuse. A report had been prepared by Lord Justice Wall in response to a report from the Women's Aid Federation of England (WAFE) about children who had been harmed by their fathers during contact visits.[23]

[22] Every Child Matters, Cm 5860, 2003.

[23] Report to the President of the Family Division on the Publication of Twenty Nine Child Homicides, 2006, by Lord Justice Wall available on http://www.judiciary.gov.uk/Resources/JCP/Documents/report_Childhomicides.pdf.

Twenty-nine had died in the previous decade, three of whom had been subject to court orders permitting unsupervised overnight contact in cases in which there had been domestic violence concerns.

The White Paper published in 2005 set out, as its title indicates, the action proposed, stressing the need for parents to minimise conflict, and setting out to provide ways of helping parents to do so. The Paper focused on what children need and how parents might be helped to meet those needs. The suggestions were intended to help all parents, though it focused mainly on the 10 per cent who need the help of the courts. The government promised to support the provision of better information and advice services; to produce parenting plans as a practical tool to help with planning contact visits; accreditation for family lawyers; national in-court conciliation schemes; better case management of the cases that do reach court; and improved judicial continuity and reduced delay.

At every stage in the preparation of the Bill difficulties arose about the precise nature and purpose of each suggestion, with those supporting the fathers seeking to maximise the benefit of any proposal to them, and those concerned to treat each case on the facts taking a different view. For example, we have discussed above how the parenting plans were originally intended to provide neutral examples of the ways in which separated parents manage contact in different circumstances. But in discussion the plans often verged into exemplars of the different situations, and questions were raised about whether these plans should be prescriptive or even mandatory.

Another example of the crucial importance of the precise terms being used in policy refinement, even before the drafting legislation, can be seen in the discussions of the recommendation that there should be contact between child and resident parents 'where it is safe and in the best interests of the child to do so' or 'where it is safe to do so'. These two formulations look very similar but are in fact a world apart. Every word has serious implications. If the formulation is restricted to simply 'safe' to do so, this is in effect a very narrow restriction on parental contact, excluding or supervising only the parents who are thought to put their children at risk of harm. But if 'in the best interests of the child' is added to 'safe' this can be interpreted as far more restrictive of parental contact, perhaps even implying that it must be demonstrated that contact would positively benefit the child (which, as research has shown, is not always the case). This latter approach sits well with the Children Act view of state intervention in the family, whereby court orders are to be made only when it will be of benefit to the child to do so. This is known as the 'no order presumption'. Those arguing to remove 'best interests' in regulating contact argued that as the welfare of the child is the basic premise of the Children Act, it was not necessary to reiterate it. Those who were afraid for children at risk of having contact against their wishes though not at risk of physical harm, wished to keep it in whichever draft was being prepared.

In the shorthand that develops among a team working on a matter day by day, when familiar and oft-used phrases become abbreviated for convenience, the words 'best interests' were often excluded, and it was not always clear whether by design or by accident. Some officials were careful to put the words back whenever they disappeared from a note or draft. Others were less concerned to do so, either because they were not sensitised to the importance of the words or because they preferred the alternative view and were content to take no action and let it roll forward. The challenge for officials in preparing the minutes of these meetings, at which the level of misunderstanding between ministers and officials was sometimes substantial, cannot be underestimated.

Responses to the consultation paper came in during the autumn of 2005, and the Bill was then drafted. The role of research remained prominent throughout the passage of the Bill through Parliament. It was ably introduced by Baroness Ashton for the DCA in the House of Lords, where a number of their Lordships were sympathetic to the fathers and supported the idea of a 50/50 timeshare presumption in the new law. They raised examples of fathers who were unable to see their children, including a case of a man who was allowed by the court only to send his child one postcard per year. Instead of backing down and accepting a formula, Government asked whether their Lordships knew of any other such case. When the answer was no, Baroness Ashton said that the Government too was not fully aware of how these cases worked in practice, and she suggested a research programme to examine exactly what non-resident fathers were asking for in the courts and exactly what the outcomes of their requests were.[24] Research had not only acted as a rational defence against emotionally-driven demands for law reform but was now being brought into the political arena and used in Parliamentary debate as a rational tool to prevent the Bill being pulled off course.

The passage of a bill through the House of Lords for the former Labour administration was always tense; and when Conservatives and Liberal Democrats decided to vote together, the Labour Government could be defeated. In this case the Bill was heavily debated, but few of the

[24] See J Hunt and A McLeod 'Outcomes of Applications to Court for Contact Orders after Parents' Separation and Divorce' (Ministry of Justice 2008).

amendments tabled had any impact. On going into the House of Commons, where the Government had a safe majority, there was little sustained opposition.

As the Bill offered so little to those who sought a 50/50 timesharing formula, serious efforts were made to respond to the other demands made by the fathers' groups, notably those concerned with the inability of the family courts to enforce contact orders against recalcitrant mothers. At the time the only weapons at a court's disposal were to imprison a mother for contempt of court or to change the residence of the child to the father. These draconian measures were scarcely ever used, and it was difficult to find a measure of coercion that would benefit a father while not harming the child. The Bill therefore contained clauses setting out contact activities that a court may require parents to take part in, in order to help them arrive at successful contact arrangements.

Again research came into play. Hunt and Roberts had prepared a second briefing paper on the interventions used in other jurisdictions to help parents with contact problems.[25] Australia had made enrolment in parenting programmes mandatory for those in breach of contact orders, and this option was considered in Westminster; but evaluation study by Helen Rhoades showed that as it is usually mothers who breach contact orders, they are the parents then sent to parenting education programs in Australia.[26] Not only do they have to pay to attend, but they have no interest in doing so as they believe it is the fathers who need the education, not themselves. While this model was therefore rejected here, the Family Resolutions Pilot (FRP) programme (described above) did go ahead. The programme was evaluated, and it was discovered that the parents who had attended found the intervention helpful, particularly the opportunity to see how parental separation looks from a child's perspective. Although the scope of the evaluation was limited because of the low take-up of the programme, the small number of parents who attended not only showed a propensity to come to agreement (as they do in other forms of in court conciliation) but were also better able to work together as parents subsequently.[27] As the report indicates ,this had not been achieved in other programmes.

[25] Hunt and Roberts, 'Intervening in Litigated Contact: Ideas from Other Jurisdictions' (above n 7).

[26] H Rhoades, 'The "No-Contact Mother": Reconstructions of Motherhood in the Era of the "New Father"' (2002) 16(1) *International Journal of Law, Policy and the Family* 71–94.

[27] L Trinder, J Kellett, J Connollyand C Notley, 'Evaluation of the Family Resolutions Pilot Project', UK Department for Education and Skills Research Report 720, 2006.

As well as helping to reach agreement between parents, the Bill also covered the issue of enforcement. A number of clauses proposing the use of electronic tagging and curfews for recalcitrant mothers were abandoned at the pre-legislative scrutiny stage; what was left in the Bill was community service penalties, which seem only minimally helpful, as they would require babysitting cover for any resident parent doing community service. The problem of enforcement therefore remains. Nonetheless, the strategy behind the Bill was to focus on getting agreements that people are comfortable with and making it easier to discuss any changes needed to arrangements, rather than expecting noncompliance to be a major problem. It is difficult to tell how successful these measures have been, as they have been slow to develop.

The Bill was passed in 2006, and there has been little activity from the fathers' groups so far. But there has also been little visible progress towards implementation.

. . .

The story of the Children and Adoption Act 2006 is one of government being pushed into responding tactically to a single-issue public campaign. Some elements in the government, including ministers, developed sympathy with the campaigning fathers. There are certainly more non-resident parents in positions of authority than there are lone mothers/parents with care. But officials and ministers looked carefully into the evidence base for policy and were not convinced of the need for formulaic regulation of contact, nor for aggressive measures to deal with non-compliant mothers. At the end of the day, the moderate, research-based view prevailed. This advocated that each case should be decided on its merits and that the Children Act should continue to provide a basic safety net for children caught up in adult disputes. Government then put its main effort into devising and supporting new ways of helping parents to manage and come through these disputes, avoiding court whenever possible.

It has been suggested that the government should go further and provide not only short-term support such as in-court conciliation but also lengthy, on-going therapeutic intervention, on the grounds that these disputes are not frivolous matters about whether a child sees his or her father on Saturday or Sunday. They are the result of deep conflict, anger and distress, which need to be dealt with if the children are to have sustainable and worthwhile relationships with both parents. These proposals would, however, require substantial resources and are unlikely to be taken further in the present period of economic stringency.

The outcome of the legislative process was basically a holding operation. The Bill was carefully drafted to maintain the Children Act approach of treating each case on its merits and putting the welfare of the child first; it avoided discussion of adult rights. There were attempts to develop ways of helping parents to agree, through contact activities, though without the kind of major investment that has occurred in Australia following their recent family law reform programme. The issue was well ventilated in Britain, but the resulting legislation carefully upheld existing policy on child law and promised little change.

We have suggested that research played a major role in producing this outcome, but there were also structural factors, such as the new government emphasis on meeting the needs of children, which manifested as a restructuring of the Department for Education and Skills, and the continuing commitment to the philosophy and terminology of the 1989 Children Act, with its emphasis on parental responsibilities rather than rights. Fathers' groups of a more moderate persuasion, notably Families need Fathers, made progress in bringing their ideas to public attention and are now firmly part of the stakeholder community that will be consulted by government in the future. But F4J, who originally enjoyed media support for their colourful antics, became more extreme and now appear to have disbanded. Any direct action involving violence is now seen in a very different light after the London bombings of 2006.

Discussion regarding what constitutes or leads to successful legislation will continue in the following chapter, but from the perspective of the policymakers, the Children and Adoption Act 2006 constituted a potentially constructive though tactical response to a highly visible but particular, single-issue campaign. It remains to be seen how the new contact activities included in the Act will develop and how helpful they will be, and also whether the extreme fathers groups will become active again. There are indications that the Coalition Government of 2010 may raise the issue again. Accusations made about gender bias in the family justice system have not been ignored by the government and are being given careful consideration in the policy work to be described in the following chapter on increasing the transparency and accountability of the courts and by the Family Justice Review. But the philosophy of the Children Act of treating each child's welfare as the paramount consideration has been upheld. The Australian experience sends out clear warning signals, and it remains to be seen whether, in the light of the negative findings from the evaluation of their recent legislation to promote shared parenting, the policy will be modified or reversed.

5

Opening up the Family Courts: The Media, the Ministry and the Children, Schools and Families Act 2010

OUR CASE STUDIES so far have described the social process of what is essentially deal-making, which underlies the passage of the major pieces of legislation affecting child law over the last 25 years in England and Wales. The first was a codifying act that was well-prepared and much wanted by specialists in the field, though of no great political interest (Children Act 1989); the second was sprung upon the public by an enthusiastic Prime Minister and carried through at speed to impose new and unpopular obligations on non-resident fathers (Child Support Act 1991); and the third was essentially an act of symbolic legislation that attempted to appease an interest group seeking access rights for fathers without giving much away (Children and Adoption Act 2006). Finally we turn to a piece of legislation that had its origins firmly within the structure of the system of Parliamentary accountability and is thereby perhaps the most democratic in origin.

Even the Children Act, the development of which saw the Law Commission playing a key role, cannot claim quite such an impeccable democratic pedigree. However, the Children Schools and Families Act may also be seen as demonstrating the somewhat Faustian price to be paid for the deals struck in the earlier pieces of legislation, which addressed public law process, child support obligations and child contact arrangements in such a way that, despite the benefits of these Acts to the children concerned, certain small but vociferous groups of adults were left feeling strongly opposed to the direction family law was taking. Mothers who felt aggrieved by decisions made by the care system and fathers who were upset by post-divorce parenting arrangements as well as increased financial demands for support were becoming increasingly critical of the family justice system. The media was more than ready to take up these causes, with loud calls for ending the 'secrecy' (or privacy) of the family courts.

In 2005 the Constitutional Affairs Select Committee (CASC), which is responsible for Parliamentary scrutiny of the Department for Constitutional Affairs (DCA), reported a lack of confidence in the family justice system and requested action. This lack of confidence had been extensively reported by the media and had been gathering pace, despite the solid foundations and clear parameters set down in the Children Act 1989. It gathered speed as a result of the complaints of fathers' groups about the perceived secrecy and bias against men in contact and residence cases, and was exacerbated by attempts to enforce aspects of the Child Support legislation that required financial contribution to each child. In private law cases fathers felt they were not being allowed sufficient access to their children, and in care cases parents were not able to discuss their cases with advisers when seeking to reverse a court judgment. Moreover, in public law cases in which the state was seeking to take on responsibility for children at risk of abuse or neglect, there had been a number of unfortunate miscarriages of justice following incomplete or inadequate evidence from medical experts. In these cases parents were distressed, in addition to being hindered in their attempts to seek better outcomes, by the limitations on discussing their cases even with other experts.

The CASC report was the start of a period of four years during which the government attempted to respond and bring forward legislation to make the family courts more open and transparent. There were varying degrees of ministerial support over this period, but the process was spurred on by relentless media activity, campaigning on its own behalf as much as on behalf of the parties directly concerned. The final outcome, after lengthy consultation and what we might call a re-consultation, which overturned the first consultation, was the passing of a Bill by a small majority in the very last days of the Parliamentary session, in a procedure known as 'wash up', after the general election had been called for May 2010.

The Children, Schools and Families Act 2010 is now on the statute book. Chapter 26 Part 2 of the Act is entitled 'Family Proceedings', but there is as yet no certainty about if or when the Act will be commenced. The changes to access and reporting rules are divided into stages, and implementation is further limited by conditions relating to a review that must demonstrate the success of the first part before moving on to the second. The Act is thus part of a strange story, one about the press not so much calling attention to a social problem as making demands in their own interests – better opportunities to find and sell exciting human interest stories. At the same time, however, greater transparency also clearly has a role to play in the liberal agenda of openness and accountability in the justice system, and it in theory complements the Parliamentary procedures for departmental scrutiny.

Background

In England and Wales family proceedings have traditionally been held in private, unlike criminal matters, which are heard in public. This is because family courts deal with matters that are private to the individuals involved; and the welfare of the children often requires that they are protected. When public debate about the reform of the law relating to parental contact began in 2005, the positions was as follows: hearings in the Court of Appeal – which is not a trial court where parties and witnesses play an active role were and remain public. In the trial courts, Magistrates Family Proceedings Court, the County Court and the High Court, cases concerning children were mainly held in private, though judges had discretion to permit the public and press to attend court when hearing financial applications relating to children and disputes over children; and the magistrates courts (Family Proceedings Courts dealing with family matters) have always been open, though seldom attended.

However, access is different from a right to report what has been observed in a courtroom. It had long been an offence in England and Wales to publish any material that would allow a child to be identified to any section of the public, and it would be counted contempt of court to release information about the substance of a case concerning a child that was held in private. However, in 2004 a CASC report on the working of the family courts expressed concerns about the need for greater public scrutiny of court proceedings, as well as the need to protect the courts from allegations of secrecy and unfairness due to decisions being made behind closed doors.[1] The CASC suggested that the press and public should be allowed into family courts, with appropriate restriction on what might be reported, subject to the discretion of the court to exclude

[1] House of Commons Constitutional Affairs Select Committee 'Freedom of Information Act: Progress towards Implementation' " Final Report of Session 2004–5,Vol 1 November 2004.

the public. The report asked that anonymised judgments should be delivered in court unless the court made an order to the contrary, and the press should continue to be restricted to publishing only matters made public by the court.

The ensuring debates became known as the transparency debate, with two major points of contention: who should be allowed into the courtrooms? And what should they be allowed to report? Some argued that allowing the press into court, even if reporting restrictions remained in force, would allow the press in some way to act as proxy witnesses for the public, thereby allaying public anxiety about bias and secrecy and improving public confidence in the justice system. Others felt that the press would not be interested in attending court if they were not able to publish items about identifiable individuals of interest to their local communities. It was also suggested that written information about decisions made in court should be given to the parties at the end of proceedings to improve their understanding of what had happened and why, instead of relying on lawyers to summarise oral judgments for their clients. At the time, transcripts of some cases in the Court of Appeal and the High Court were being anonymised and published in the law reports, as well as on a website run by the charity British and Irish Legal Information Institute (BAILII).

The Consultation Processes

In September 2005 the Department of Constitutional Affairs (DCA, now Ministry of Justice (MoJ)) asked Maclean to host a roundtable discussion in Oxford with judges, lawyers, academics, officials, representatives of children associations, and psychiatrists and psychologists from a number of jurisdictions. The following issues were to be discussed:

- Should family courts continue to be held in private, or should public and media access be wider under the new unified court system?
- How can judgments be used to improve the openness of family courts?
- How are vulnerable children and adults best protected?

Although the Department was required to respond to the recommendations of the CASC, which was responsible for scrutinising their work for Parliament, they were unsure of how widespread these concerns were and how the professionals in the field and the other stakeholders would respond. The aim of the meeting was therefore to gain impressions of these in order to inform the early work for ministers on the feasibility and desirability of change.

Public and private law cases relating to children were to be considered at the meeting; financial matters and adoption were to be excluded for the time being. A range of detailed points for discussion were set out by the Department. Participants were asked whether they thought courts should be open, with discretion to close them; or whether they should be closed, with discretion to open them. The gravity of the decisions being taken was emphasised to the participants, with the possibility of children being taken from their parents in circumstances they did not necessarily understand. If that is the case, it is important that not only the individual parents but also society as a whole understands the kinds of decisions being made and the reasons for them.

The DCA background papers for the Oxford meeting acknowledged the tension between the rights of the children involved; the freedom of the press (ie, between justice being done and being seen to be done); and the right of families to privacy. The need to find out about the views of young people on the matter was emphasised. It was also pointed out that the question of access by the press and public and the question of reporting restrictions needed to be looked at separately. A warning was issued about the resource implications of trying to provide anonymised written judgments in all cases. And finally it was suggested that transparency might require full access, even if people do not want others present at discussions of their family matters.

The stakeholders who met in Oxford in September 2005 were unanimous in their opposition to the idea of making courts open yet subject to discretion to close, as well as to any increase in reporting. There was, however, interest in the idea of having more written anonymised judgments, to act as sources of information for the children in later life. If a child were to grow to adulthood without seeing one or both parents, the child should have access to the decision made by the court and the reasons for that decision as of right. But there was also concern about women who had experienced violence and about whether access by press or public might affect the willingness of parties, including those from ethnic minority backgrounds, to take part in court proceedings.

Transparency was clearly a serious and multifaceted issue, and not confined to England and Wales. At this first exploratory meeting, participants were also informed about the position in Australia and the recent changes in New Zealand. Australia had experienced unrestricted state-level access to courts in the 1960s, and this had led to sensationalist reporting of family cases. The 1975 Family Law Act reversed the position, making family hearings private. But the Act was amended in 1983 to create once again a more open system. The change came about because perceptions of secrecy and the questioning of decisions in the press undermined the courts, a situation somewhat analogous to what had been happening in the United Kingdom prior to the Children, Schools and Families Act 2010. As a consequence of the 1983 amendments in Australia the public were given the right to attend court, but after a brief flurry of interest, few people did so.

In Australia the Family Court starts from the principle that proceedings shall be heard in open court, but section 97 of the Family Law Act 1983, as amended, also allows for hearings by a judge or magistrate sitting in chambers, and allocates wide discretionary powers to courts to determine who can attend court hearings. The Court can of its own volition grant the request of any party and order that part or all of a hearing is to be held in private. Legislation in some states specifically excludes the press in Children and Juvenile Courts, and in others permits press and other attendance but retains wide discretionary powers to hear cases in private. The system seems to work well, as publishing restrictions are tightly managed and are respected by the press. Judges have a similar discretion to restrict access to both press and public, but because the press respect the limitations and are mindful of the sanctions for any breach, there is rarely any need for judicial intervention.

There are also clear guidelines on how to anonymise judgments. The penalties under section 21 of the Family Law Act prevent the press from printing certain information and carry a one-year custodial sentence for serious transgressions. No one as yet has been sent to prison. On the other hand, the limitations on what can be reported are so restrictive that very little information can be published, and this dissuades the press from attending court. Reporting for professionals and law students is done anonymously and with additional information included, and this is encouraged by the courts.

New Zealand recently dealt with access to courts in the Care of Children Act (COCA) 2004, which does not permit members of the general public to attend unless given permission by the relevant judge. The act does permit accredited news media to attend, but this is qualified by judicial discretion to exclude reporters during a hearing.

Following the initial meeting in Oxford in 2005 and despite the universally critical response from the stakeholders present, DCA Ministers in 2006 proceeded to a consultation exercise, based on the document

'Confidence and Confidentiality: Improving Transparency and Privacy in Family Courts'.[2] The proposals put out for consultation would allow the press to attend court hearings on behalf of and for the benefit of the public, though the court could exclude them and direct reporting restrictions; others would be allowed to attend on application; and a new criminal offence would be created for breach of reporting restrictions, which would ensure the anonymity of children and adults, though these restrictions could be relaxed or increased by a court; and finally, rules would be made consistent across all the family courts and proceedings. At that time the distinctions between the different courts and different proceedings were causing confusion and adding to press hostility.

The DCA also began to look into the current practice of the courts, for example, asking how frequently judges or magistrates record their decisions and the reasons for them and whether this is done on tape or in notebooks. Inquiries found that judgments are usually given verbally immediately after a hearing, as opposed to being written out and then read in court; judgments are recorded as spoken unless the order is agreed; and recordings are kept for three years.

The DCA had published already in July 2005 the response to the earlier, more specific consultation exercise.[3] 57 responses had been received from members of the judiciary, courts, voluntary organisations, academics and private individuals. Some progress in relaxing restrictions had already been made through changes to the rules of court, to enable families to seek advice and support.

In October 2006 the consultation process continued with a small group of stakeholders at a 'Day of Perspectives', at which key stakeholder representatives were asked to give their views on the proposals within 'Confidence and Confidentiality'. This meeting, chaired by Maclean, was located in the Bunker, the underground cabinet war rooms from World War II in St James Park, under the Chatham House convention by which comments may be repeated outside the meeting but not attributed without consent. There was some amusement at the meeting about the DCA sense of what is appropriate – in this case, to discuss openness and transparency for the courts in what has historically been the most restricted location in London.

[2] Department for Constitutional Affairs (DCA), *Confidence and Confidentiality: Improving Transparency and Privacy in Family Courts* (Consultation paper 11/06, Cm 6886, 2006).

[3] Department for Constitutional Affairs (DCA), 'Disclosure of Information in Family Proceedings Cases involving Children: Response to the Public Consultation' (Cm 6623, 2005).

At the meeting a variety of views were strongly expressed. The Family Bar representative was supportive of the principle of openness and quoted a Strasbourg ruling in *De Haes and Gijsels v Belgium*:

> The press plays a preeminent role in a state governed by the rule of law . . . The press is one of the means by which politicians and public opinion can verify that judges are discharging their heavy responsibilities in a manner in conformity with the aim which is the basis of the task entrusted to them.[4]

The Family Bar representative supported greater harmonisation of rules across the different tiers of court structure, saying also that interested parties should generally be given access. But he did not feel that it was necessary either to promote the public interest in the administration of justice or to contradict misinformation that the media should be present throughout the whole of family proceedings. He therefore supported judicial discretion about attendance but full public access at the point of delivery of judgment, which should be anonymised to protect the identity of children.

Meanwhile, a representative of the fathers' groups took a far more robust position in defence of greater openness. He stated:

> A heavy onus of proof should be on those who wish to have any aspect of the hearings in secret and not to be divulged. Of course, that case will be made on occasion, but they are the ones that need justifying. Some of the arguments for secrecy do not stand up to examination. Openness would improve the quality of the work done in the courts.

A representative from the media went even further, demanding total openness and freedom to report, comparing the current position in the United Kingdom to that in the Republic of North Korea. However, a judge reminded those present of the local nature of these kinds of cases and sought to protect the privacy of families and to avoid local people putting together separate anonymised items of information to achieve jigsaw-recognition of particular children. This argument was taken further by medical experts, who described how any limitation on their ability to assure those whom they assess for the court of the confidentiality of the process would not only infringe their medical code of ethical practice but also have the practical effect of reducing the willingness of the parties to cooperate in the process.

The impassioned opening speech from the Minister responsible for family justice, Harriet Harman, in favour of greater openness was received with enthusiasm only by the press representatives and members of the

[4] *De Haes and Gijsels v Belgium* (1997) 25 EHHR 1, para 37.

fathers' groups whose criticisms of the family justice system had contributed to the views expressed by the Select Committee. The sense of the meeting as a whole remained cautious.

The officials took away the following messages and continued to work on detailed proposals along these lines: the need for greater openness and transparency in the family courts was agreed, as was the need for consistency across the courts; but there was a call for clarity of detail on the proposal being put forward and perhaps a need for gradual introduction of any change. The focus of any change should be on improving the quality of and improving confidence in the family justice system, which could be helped by greater inspection, peer review and research. Concerns remained for the safety of victims of domestic violence and abuse, as well as witnesses. There was also continuing concern about anonymity, as well as a lack of confidence in the press and suggestions for an accreditation system.

In March 2007 the DCA published the responses to the 2006 consultation, showing a new emphasis on building confidence in the justice system.[5] These responses showed strong support for making more information available on the workings of the justice system, especially for those involved in proceedings. There was particular interest in the proposal on later life information, that is, information to be retained for adults about family proceedings in which they had been involved as children. Children and young people in their responses agreed that later life information should be available and that this could take a variety of forms, such as transcripts or summaries of judgments.

However, a number of responses were concerned about the attendance of the media in court and stressed the need to prioritise the welfare of the children and young people the justice system exists to protect. There was scepticism about the ability to maintain anonymity if any reporting is allowed, as well as concern that children who are the subjects of proceedings may be upset by the presence of others in court. The responses from the media were, unsurprisingly, more optimistic. The views of the Children and Family Court Advisory and Support Service (CAFCASS) Children Panel were especially powerful in their argument that the children themselves should say whether their case should be heard in private.

A subsequent expert seminar arranged by the Nuffield Foundation in April 2007 was also critical of the developing policy, with concerns being raised by the senior judiciary about the need to protect children.

[5] Department for Constitutional Affairs (DCA), *Confidence and Confidentiality: Improving Transparency and Privacy in Family Courts* (response to consultation CP(R) 11/06, Cm 7036, 2007).

These consultation findings were not welcome to the Ministers of the day, who sought to move ahead in the direction of more openness, both to comply with the requests of the Select Committee and also in order to earn some positive reaction from the press. But the reservations expressed about the direction of policy, especially those from organisations working with children, were disquieting. The decision was taken to hold a second consultation exercise, with a new approach, which began in June 2007.

The 2007 consultation paper was entitled 'Confidence and Confidentiality: Openness in the Family Courts – A New Approach'.[6] This paper reversed the proposal to allow media access to courts as of right, instead making the interesting suggestion that it is the information that comes out of the courts which can improve understanding of and confidence in the courts, not who physically enters the court. This formulation of the idea had been supported by the special adviser to the then Lord Chancellor, Lord Falconer, and was firmly grounded in the principle that the children must come first. The paper emphasised that better information should be provided:

- in cases involving children and adults in proceedings;
- to a wider public about decisions in cases in which there is an element of public interest.

The provision of information to parents and others about the decisions in their own cases was to be piloted, and there would be a new source of online information about family courts.

This consultation paper went further in protecting the anonymity of children after proceedings had closed than the current legal position, but at the same time, it proposed making the rules on disclosure less restrictive and for the first time began to include adoption proceedings in the plans for change.

Detailed Policy Work: Moving Slowly Forward

As officials turned to the detailed proposals for change, the development of the policy became more complex and conflicted. Children's organisations, lawyers and doctors became increasingly opposed to the plans for

[6] Ministry of Justice (MoJ), *Confidence and Confidentiality: Openness in Family Courts – A New Approach* (Consultation paper CP 10/07, Cm 7173, 2007).

more transparency as the detail began to emerge. Even the senior judiciary, including the present President of the Family Division, Lord Justice Wall, who had originally welcomed moves to make their work more visible and thus hopefully see a better and understanding of the complexity of their work, especially in child protection, began to feel uncomfortable. The expert seminar held by the Nuffield Foundation had raised further criticism of the direction of policy. The gap between expert views on the one hand and the demands of the press for access to the courts on the other widened, with government sitting uncomfortably in between. The then Lord Chancellor, Lord Falconer, was well versed in family law and understood the expert concerns. But his junior Minister, Harriet Harman, had a passionate personal commitment to greater openness. Her sister, Sarah Harman, was a practising family solicitor who had been involved in a case in which a parent had been accused of abuse; and though the evidence given by an expert had been questioned, the restrictions on sharing information in such cases had made it difficult for the parent to seek redress, and Sarah Harman, as her solicitor had been disciplined by the profession for breach of these rules when trying to help her client.

As this legislative enterprise moved slowly forward, the mix of public and private motivations and interaction became more and more intriguing. As we have suggested above, the apparent source of concern leading to this project came from the most propitious of sources, the Constitutional Affairs Select Committee, which is charged with consideration of the working of the justice system – an impeccably democratic source for legislative reform. But the Select Committee's views were heavily influenced by the pressure group promoting the concerns of fathers who felt they had been poorly treated in their applications to the courts for greater access to their children.[7] Any public concern must be considered by CASC, but the 'capture' by the issue of media attention was also a factor. Subsequent research has shown the fathers' concerns about bias in contact and residence cases to be without foundation.[8]

When Harman, a Minister with great ability and energy as well as a personal agenda, entered the scene, the thrust for legislation became a powerful one. In the midst of it, officials doggedly pursued the detailed work of consultation with experts, stakeholders and those potentially affected by the proposals (especially the children). In attempting to find detailed alternative ways of moving the matter forward, they inevitably

[7] See above ch 3.

[8] J Hunt and A Macleod, 'Outcomes of Applications to the Courts for Contact Orders after Parental Separation or Divorce' (policy report for the Ministry of Justice, 2008).

failed to satisfy the Minister but also attracted opprobrium from those with expert knowledge. This is an unenviable position to be in but not unusual for a public servant. The irony is that here the most democratic of stimuli for action was also the most vulnerable to capture by pressure groups, as the Committee interests coincided with the personal interests of the media.

In December 2008, the DCA, now renamed the Ministry of Justice (MoJ), published a reassessment of the responses to the second consultation paper, together with a new proposal from government, following the appointment of a new Secretary of State for Justice, Jack Straw.[9] The overriding principle of the 2007 consultation paper of putting children first had been replaced by three new principles, which were to be taken as standing together:

1. to improve confidence in the family courts, which was alleged to have been failing;
2. to protect the interests of children and vulnerable adults; and
3. to enable more lay support for adults in court.

These principles would require primary legislation and would allow the press into family courts unless a court decided against it in the interests of the children or for the safety and protection of the adults. Public information about court procedures was to be increased. Some anonymised judgments were to be placed online on the BAILII website as part of a pilot programme entitled the Family Court Information Pilot, so that members of the public could see what decisions are made and how. Also as part of the pilot programme, parties were to be given a copy of any judgment in their own cases made so that they could have a record. A consistent set of reporting restrictions was to be provided to protect families and to clarify what information cannot be published without the permission of the court. Provision for protecting a child's identity after the closing of a case was to be made, and it would become possible for parties to disclose case information for the purpose of seeking advice, support or mediation, and for onward disclosure to others to be made with the permission of the party making the disclosure. Anonymised information was to be made available for training and research purposes.

This change of direction was justified by the results of the consultation, in which there was little support for the views that the press should never or always be allowed into court; but 85 per cent of those responding had said that a court should be able to exclude if appropriate.

[9] Ministry of Justice (MoJ) *Family Justice in View* Response to Consultation 16/07 Cm7502 2008.

The new guidelines for media access to the courts came into effect in April 2009, but primary legislation remained a matter for conjecture.

Progress?

When the second consultation response was published, it was four years since the first recommendations of the Parliamentary Select Committee. What had been accomplished in this time? Those seeking greater openness – men complaining about post-divorce parenting decisions; women concerned about the way they had been criticised in a small number of child protection cases and prevented from referring documents on to advisers; and the media – had made a strong start in their campaign.

Demands for freedom, openness, scrutiny of secretive processes, consistency between courts and improvements to the justice system have great resonance, and as general statements, they are hard to contest. Few from the legal world expressed reservations at the early stages. However, concerns had been raised from the beginning by those working with or representing children, that their privacy must be protected. And from the medical side, patient confidentiality had inevitably always been a serious issue.

Meanwhile, officials continued the detailed work of identifying the discrepancies between current court practices and setting out the precise circumstances in which the media might attend, which members might attend and what they might record and publish, as well as whether they should have access to documents or simply be allowed to listen to what is said in court (which is only a small part of the presentation of a case). As they did so, a number of new issues emerged, with the overall impact of increasing the concerns held by those working in the system. Those whose interests and experience lay at a distance from the process remained sanguine, including the press themselves and the pressure groups with a case to make. But the judges, lawyers, social workers and, in particular, the medical professions working in the courts became more and more troubled. At the same time Ministerial enthusiasm for action increased. Serious tensions therefore developed as the government began to indicate a commitment to early primary legislation.

For example, Harriet Harman began to discuss whether adoption proceedings should be held in public. It was suggested that if people must marry in public under English law, surely they should adopt in public.

Social workers and child specialists were horrified at the lack of regard for the privacy of adoptive parents and adopted children. Lawyers were upset by the lack of appreciation of the two legal stages in adoption proceedings following a care order. If a child is to be taken from parents who are unable to provide acceptable care, the Local Authority Social Services Department will ask for the child to be freed for adoption. This is a complex legal process, with many safeguards for the rights of biological parents, and it could arguably be subject to public scrutiny. But an actual adoption itself, whereby a child moves to the adoptive parents, has always been regarded in this jurisdiction as private to the adoptive parents and child. Article 8 of the European Convention of Human Rights provides a right to respect for private and family life. Interference is permissible in accordance with domestic law in some circumstances, for example to protect a child, but it must be proportionate and temporary. Neither of these factors pertains in the circumstances of adoption proceedings. Indeed, Article 6(1), which provides for a fair and public hearing within a reasonable time and for public pronouncement of judgments, is qualified in that it allows for the exclusion of the press from all or part of a trial when the interests of juveniles or the protection of the private life of the parties so require.

Those working in the courts became increasingly anxious not only about safety issues where domestic violence or forced marriage is an issue but also about the impact on court evidence if parties or witnesses are afraid of being identified. Would parties feel confident to use the courts to deal with their problems at all? Concerns continued about the local impact of press access and reporting, even with strict anonymisation procedures; and what is termed 'jigsaw recognition' (whereby someone with local knowledge might piece together the identity of an otherwise unnamed child simply by putting together a number of separate items of information such as age, number of siblings, school attended, etc) was raised again as a serious issue.

There had been a lengthy period of development work, not unusual when officials find it hard to produce a proposal to satisfy a ministerial call for action when they know that the experts and practitioners in the field are strongly opposed to the direction being taken. By the summer of 2009, the Labour Administration had been in power for twelve years. Popularity was waning, Gordon Brown's premiership, after the initial honeymoon period, was attracting harsh press criticism on many fronts, including family justice. The Secretary of State for Justice Jack Straw was visited a number of times over the summer by a journalist named Camilla Cavendish, who had run a series of articles over the summer in

The Times newspaper criticising the secretive nature of the family courts.[10] Her work was rewarded with a journalistic award, and her ideas were enthusiastically received by the Secretary of State: here might be a way for a beleaguered government to achieve some press appreciation while at the same supporting the high principles of openness and accountability. Jack Straw hence demanded action. A bill was to be prepared to enable the press to attend an expanded group of cases and to report the substance of cases as long as the parties and children were not identified; some sensitive personal information would be excluded, but expert witnesses, including doctors, were to be named.

Public announcements were made on 27 April and 9 July. The work was to be taken forward by MoJ officials, together with the Department for Children, Schools and Families (DCSF), which has responsibility for all services for children. Interestingly, there were difficulties in reaching an agreed position between the two government departments. The DCSF not surprisingly listened with more sympathy to the views of the groups working with children and were critical of the speed with which the plans for legislation were being moved forward and of the apparent failure to give priority to the welfare of children. The first draft Bill prepared by officials took into account these views of the DCSF but was rejected by the Secretary of State for Justice. He required a second draft, to reflect his views more accurately and to be much clearer about extending both media access and limiting reporting restrictions. This was prepared by the Parliamentary draftsmen but was subsequently not found acceptable by the DCSF Minster, Ed Balls. Neither ministers nor their special advises could agree a compromise, and the problem was handed back to officials. With consummate skill, they produced a third draft Bill, which divided the process into two stages, giving hope to those opposing the measure that before the second, more draconian stage could be reached, an election would be called. Opposition views of the Bill were critical at this stage. One of the concerns being voiced was the extraordinary haste with which the matter was being pursued.

The Bill as published included the following provisions:

> With the aim of producing a family justice system that is transparent, accountable, and inspires public confidence in its good work, whilst protecting the privacy of the children and families involved, a two stage bill is proposed. Stage 1 would be implemented straight away, and stage 2 after a delay of at least 18 months during which there should be a review of stage 1 and the conclusions of that review should be laid before Parliament.

[10] See, for example, *The Times*, 9 July 2009.

Stage 1 would continue the present position on media attendance at court hearings but would expand the range of cases open to the media. There would be no change concerning access to documents, but the children and their families in court cases would have lifelong anonymity, unless a court said otherwise. The media could report the substance of the cases they saw if a number of conditions were met, but some sensitive information would be on a banned list. Experts paid by a court could be named, but others would have their identity protected. Anyone could publish an anonymised version of the text or summary of a court order, except in adoption cases, but court judgments could not be reported unless the court specifically allowed it, and the sanction for breach would remain contempt of court.

Stage 1 represents the moderate views originally presented by MoJ officials, which were acceptable to the Department of Children Schools and Families (DCSF), previously DfES). Stage 2 represents the further changes required by Jack Straw, and later accepted by DCSF, with the expectation that they would have no certainty of reaching implementation given the widespread opposition to the Bill and the imminence of a general election and change of Government.

The second stage would remove the category of banned sensitive personal information and remove restrictions on the naming of expert witnesses. Although the plans to make further changes to the law were announced in April 2009, no details were published until the Bill itself appeared in November 2010. The reason for this was that there was no agreement about what the Bill would contain before that date.

On publication of the Bill, strong concerns were immediately expressed by the Interdisciplinary Alliance for Children and the Family Justice Council, as well as by judges, doctors and family law experts. These concerns were not fully reported by the media. The major concerns were about the speed with which the government was pushing ahead with these fundamental changes, which meant that results of the pilot scheme for publishing anonymised judgments online were not yet available; moreover, it was felt that there was no consideration of why privacy was being put at risk in this way and no discussion of the resource implications.

There was also no discussion of the distinction between anonymity and privacy. For example, Robert George with Ceridwen Roberts have cited a story published in the *Daily Mail* on 20 November 2009 involving a case in which the Family Court had moved a child from his mother to his father.[11] The newspaper did not report the details of the parents or

[11] RH George with C Roberts, 'The Media and the Family Courts: Key Information and Questions about the Children, Schools and Families Bill', Family Policy Briefing Paper 6 (University of Oxford Department of Social Policy and Social Work, 2009).

their disputes but did give the father's marital status, his home county and the size and cost of his house. Although the general public would not be able to identify him, it is quite probable that people in the same locality might well do so. What purpose was being served by publishing these details? In contrast, if a journalist had attended the case in family court and then had access to an anonymised judgment, he or she would be have been well placed to report effectively on the proceedings.

The proposals in the Bill together went far beyond both the degree of openness provided under recent changes in New Zealand and the long-standing position in Australia.[12] The Children, Schools and Families Bill was brought before Parliament in the very last days of the Brown administration and seemed likely to be lost when the Parliamentary session ended. But there is a process called 'wash up', through which the party officials known as Whips, who manage Parliamentary business for government and opposition, meet to decide which Bills should be expedited before Parliamentary business is concluded. The clauses relating to the courts and media were a small part of the Children, Schools and Families Bill, which deals largely with matters relating to schools, and Jack Straw was most anxious that it should be included in the wash up.

Despite substantial and weighty opposition, including speeches in the House of Lords from a former Lord Chancellor (Lord Mackay of Clashfern) and a former President of the Family Division (Lady Elizabeth Butler Sloss), the Bill scraped through with a small majority and became law in April 2010. The provisions were as described above, with one key amendment, which secured the support of members of the opposition. Due to the amendment, stage 2 would not be activated until at least 18 months after commencement of the Act and would furthermore be dependent on a review of the Family Court Information (Anonymised Judgments) Pilot, to be put before Parliament by the Secretary of State for Justice.

The Coalition Government now in office at the time of writing (September 2010) has not yet made any announcements about implementation of the new legislation. Although there was some Conservative support for the Bill, it was not unanimous or strongly expressed. The Liberal Democrats are sympathetic to greater openness in the family justice system but were cautious about the issue of protecting children. The Coalition Government is in a difficult position: any move towards implementation

[12] See J Brophy with C Roberts, 'Openness and Transparency in Family Courts: What the Experience of Other Countries Tells Us about Reform in England and Wales', Family Policy Briefing Paper 5 (University of Oxford Department of Social Policy and Social Work, 2009); and George with Roberts (ibid).

would arouse a storm of protest from experts in the field, as doctors, lawyers, judges and social workers, who each have their own concerns, all feel the need to protect children and have questioned the rapidity of such drastic changes, which is unparalleled in other jurisdictions. On the other hand, any announcement of delay by the Coalition Government or any move to repeal the legislation would arouse a storm of protest from the media, who already feel that the planned changes do not go far enough to support the freedom of the press.

There is one relatively safe option. The previous Administration announced and the Coalition has continued a fundamental review of the family justice system. A Review Panel, chaired by David Norgrove, is looking not at substantive family law but at the workings of courts and lawyers and their administration. Since no report will be released earlier than the end of 2011, a prudent option might be for the government to delay any decision until this report has been published and considered. This might be feasible, as the pilot scheme for anonymised judgments is planned to run until the end of 2010, and a report on this is a formal part of the process. The stringent economic measures being taken by the government following the economic crisis make the survival of even this modest pilot scheme a matter for conjecture. Its chances of survival may be improved by allowing the government to give the appearance of trying to promote openness and transparency without actually taking forward the other aspects of the Children Schools and Families Act.

A Success?

If little change occurs as a result of the Children, Schools and Families Act, the time, civil service resources and additional court-based work that was involved in the development process may be hard to justify. On the other hand, there are those who would see this as a cheap price to pay for avoiding changes that could damage the welfare of children who are already going through the difficult experience of family proceedings.

If the pilot scheme for anonymised judgments, which is currently running in only two county courts and three family proceedings courts, becomes the total output of the five-year attempt to legislate the opening-up of family courts, how do we evaluate the process and result? We must remember that it was the Parliamentary Select Committee that asked for review and reform of the family court system in order to reduce secrecy and bias. A serious accusation was made, even though it may have been unduly influenced by a small group of activists for fathers' rights following the failed attempt to overturn the system for post-separation parenting in the Children and Adoption Act 2006. Government was required to take up the issue, and a team of experienced officials was set to work, producing a soundly researched consultation exercise. The findings of the first consultation contradicted the direction the government wished to take towards opening up the courts, and a second consultation was launched with a slightly different focus on increasing the amount of information coming out of the courts rather than looking at who was entitled to enter.

There is a great gulf between allowing media access and allowing reporting, as well as an important distinction to be made between privacy and anonymity. The new proposals attempted to deal with both of these carefully and constructively. But at that moment, press involvement suddenly became active and high-profile. *The Times* began its campaign,[13] capturing the support of a vulnerable minister at a time when the government was in serious difficulties with the press and approaching an election. The result was that the Secretary of State began to make faster and more extensive demands for change and, after confrontation with ministerial colleagues at DCSF, succeeded in putting to Parliament a strong form of words, which were not in any way commensurate with the findings of either consultation exercise. Legislation has been rushed onto the statute book after a long and complex consultation history, but remains a long way from implementation In the case studies in the three previous chapters, we focussed on legislative work in the sense of identifying issues, working on building support and the technical drafting and implementation of legislation. In this case it may be of interest to give a more detailed account of the nature and extent of the preparatory work required from government and courts in order for change to take place. If we take the more popular aspects of the pilot scheme for anonymised judgments programme for change – the attempts to provide better information to parties and to improve public confidence in the system – the story is complex and costly. This part of the programme developed into the Family Court Information Pilot which began in 2009. The task required careful definition at regular meetings by an advisory group made up of senior and junior judiciary, officials, representatives of the DCFS, CAFCASS, the National Society for the Prevention of Cruelty to Children (NSPCC) and experts.[14] This group

[13] See above regarding Camilla Cavendish's articles in *The Times*.

[14] Maclean was a member of this group.

had to set out which cases should be covered by the programme, what information should be made available and how it should be collected.

At an early planning meeting in 2009 it became apparent that in many cases involving children, there is no adjudication as such; instead, a court makes an order by consent for the parties. In these cases there is no judgment to be given, and none will be recorded. So the advisory group asked if the judiciary might prepare a summary account of any decision that has been taken in a contested case and the reasons for the decision. This was not difficult for the Family Proceedings Courts, where the magistrates have always been required to record their decisions and the reasons for them. But in the county courts, judges may simply say that an order had been made as requested, or they may give oral but not written judgments. Even when transcribed, these judgments might not help the parties involved understand the decision. For example, a judgment might say no more than that the judge was persuaded by the arguments put forward in bundle 3, paragraph 37. Even with careful transcription and redaction, with the anonymisation process carefully safeguarded by the scrutiny of judge and parties or their lawyers, it is hard to see how this kind of document could either improve the parties understanding of the work of the courts or improve the level of confidence of the general public in the justice system.

When consulted, judges said that if they were to write more judgments, and do so in ways that would be helpful to parties or to the children concerned, it would take time – and judicial time is a scarce resource. Any additional work would mean additional delay in listing new cases. Similarly, the issuing of later-life judgments, which was the only idea in the original pilot programme of 2009 to receive universal support, would be extremely difficult for courts to put into practice.

Everyone agreed that a child who had been the subject of a care order and taken from his or her parents should, on reaching adulthood, have access to a document that explains why the decision was taken. But who would write such a document? Who would safely store it? How would a child know where to look for it on reaching age 16 or 18 or whichever age is thought to be appropriate? Would there be any support for young adults making these inquiries, as there is in the case of adopted adults seeking birth parents? Judges seemed reluctant to try to write any kind of summary (in case of appeal) or any document that was not a judgment. Furthermore, it was argued that social services departments already hold a file on each child, containing copies of court orders and all other relevant information, and a child can access this with the support of a social worker when it is thought appropriate. The proposals for later-life judgments therefore fell away.

The pilot project advisory group were left with the task of persuading courts to take part in the pilot, with the result that participation in the pilot meant that those courts had to identify the cases, write and anonymise judgments, and log the time taken by those working on these tasks in order to estimate the costs of the additional work. The transcripts of judgments within the President's definition in the pilot courts have been put on the BAILLI website, and a customer satisfaction survey has been run online to check who was using the website and whether they found it helpful. After six months, the judges and court staff were interviewed about how the project was working, and BAILLI user responses were analysed. A large number of hits were recorded on the website, mainly from social workers, Guardians ad Litem, and lawyers, including some law teachers. Very few members of the public or journalists had looked at the site. The comment of one journalist was that the site was no help to him, as it did not identify the parties. Exactly so. Lawyers found it of some interest but were already familiar with the kind of information set out. Those who found the system most beneficial were the social workers, who said that it helped them to see what the court wanted from them. Among judges, legal advisers and court staff, there was a certain amount of scepticism about the value of the work, particularly because they felt it was not really the job of the courts to train social workers; moreover, providing training materials would be much simpler.

At the end of the day a great deal of effort and stress had been required to run a small pilot scheme, which does not appear to be highly valued by those involved and very unlikely to have any impact on the parties or the general public.

This case study has presented a very proper democratic exercise that has yielded little benefit but appears costly in terms of work done by officials in preparation and time spent by stakeholders in opposition. The Polish concern with chronic legislative effort offers a parallel situation. For example, there have been repeated attempts in Poland to legislate on abortion and lustration, but there is no majority view, and agreement cannot be reached in either the Polish Parliament or within Polish society more generally. In the current UK context, we do now have a piece of legislation on the statute book. But even Westminster party discipline, which usually leads to a more controlled legislative programme, could not deal with fundamental differences of view. The circle could not be squared. There was no way to integrate the two views that transparency is good and children need privacy. Despite extensive policy work in preparation and consultation, and pilot schemes to test feasibility, confidence and confidentiality remain hard to reconcile. The outcome is yet to be seen.

6

Reflections

Introduction

We began with the aim of offering detailed case studies in family law by drawing on personal observation of the legislative process, hoping to be able to move on from the traditional rational theory of law making to offer a more empirically based socio-legal account. This was ambitious. We can present only a small number of cases, and personal observations are of course always of limited reliability, though hopefully of some interest. Nevertheless, with all due caution, in this chapter we offer some general observations in response to what we see as the underlying questions, and then try to develop issues for further consideration. A companion volume in preparation will in due course present full case studies from the Polish context, but here we will make general reference to the Polish experience, using it, as we have done in previous comparative work,[1] to hold a mirror to refract our local experience. By looking at what we do through the eyes of others we hope to become more aware of aspects that otherwise are taken for granted and see more clearly what distinguishes the law-making process in Westminster.

The questions we addressed through the case studies are as follows:

1. What do we mean by law?
2. Who takes part in the legislative process?
3. What stimulates legislative activity?
4. How is law made?
5. What legislation works well, for whom and why?

[1] See, for example, J Kurczewski and M Maclean, *Family Law and Family Policy in the New Europe*, Oñati International Series in Law and Society (Aldershot, Ashgate, 1997).

1. What Do We Mean by Law?

For this book we have limited ourselves to the creation of statute law in Parliament. We have not looked closely at state regulation, even though the extent of the law made by regulations laid before Parliament but requiring neither debate or vote in England and Wales is often underestimated.[2] State regulation was of course the dominant model in pre-1989 Poland under the Communist regime, but it is understandably no longer regarded as desirable. It will be of interest to see whether the new politics of the UK Coalition Government of 2010, which seeks to reduce the power of the state and work through the Big Society, will have any impact on the level of legislative activity through regulation.

We have also set aside law-making or statutory interpretation through judicial adjudication. Here too there are structural differences between the English and Polish jurisdictions associated with the civil and common law traditions in each country. In Poland, as in other civil law jurisdictions, any disputed point of law must be adjudicated by the Supreme or Constitutional Court, while in England and Wales, the judiciary interpret conflict arising from interpretation of statute. It is possible, however, that different uses of the terms 'adjudication' and 'interpretation' may mask a greater similarity between the jurisdictions than might be apparent to the outside world. The Supreme Court in Warsaw must 'interpret' in order to 'adjudicate', while the English judiciary must 'adjudicate' for their 'interpretations' to be visible and binding.

2. Who Takes Part in the Legislative Process? Who Makes Law?

In the United Kingdom almost all statutory change is initiated by the government and is modified and agreed by Parliament before becoming law. A government minister will select a topic, and then public officials will advise on the feasibility and desirability of the idea and, with ministerial agreement, work on the detailed plan until it is clear enough to be put into the form of instructions to the Parliamentary drafters, who will prepare a bill. This will then be guided through Parliament by the originating minister, supported by officials, until Royal Assent is given. Only a very small contribution is made by individual Members of Parliament through private members' bills. But this is not the only way of introducing legislation.

[2] See in particular with regard to the Child Support Act, above ch 3.

In Poland legal drafts come from a far wider range of sources, though the role of government is increasing. Between 2001 and 2005 in Poland 1265 laws were initiated, of which 63 per cent came from government and 29 per cent from individual members of the Sejm. The remainder came from committees, the Senate, the President or directly by petition from citizens. But we also need to be aware that members of the government in Poland, unlike in the United Kingdom, are not necessarily members of Parliament. Indeed, in other jurisdictions, Estonia for example, an elected member of Parliament is required to relinquish his or her seat on accepting a government position. The seat will then be allocated to a candidate coming next on the list for the same party in the preceding election. This raises the question of who is representing whom in the democratic legislative process. At Westminster, a Member of Parliament represents his or her local constituents but is bound by the party discipline enforced by the party whips, and the MP expects to follow the programme set out by his or her party in its election manifesto.

The British system may be described as centralised in the legislative process but open to some modification or fine-tuning in subsequent judicial interpretation. In the Polish system the sources of legislation are decentralised. There may even be two versions of a bill traveling through the parliamentary process, with government using comments on the alternative to their bill in order to draw out criticisms and manage the desired outcome. But once passed and scrutinised by the Constitutional Court, the provisions of a bill will not be modified by judicial interpretation. It seems that there is a need for flexibility at some point, whether before or after legislation has completed its parliamentary process.

3. What Stimulates Legislative Activity?

We suggest that governments generally seek to make law because they cannot achieve their objective as cost effectively in any other way, for example through information and exhortation. They may consider legislation in response to a public outcry on some issue; there may be pressure from a number of interest groups for action; there may be a longstanding, well-researched independent inquiry that identifies an issue which requires legislation; or issues may be identified by a parliamentary body responsible for scrutiny of the functions of the state. Or a minister may simply have a personal interest or be seeking to distract an electorate from other matters.

Governments in different situations will be more or less likely to legislate. For example, the Labour Government elected in 1997 was hungry for legislation. The party had been out of office for 10 years, and they had a lengthy manifesto for change that was full of promises to the electorate. They also had a large majority in the House of Commons, which made the legislative process easier to conduct. In Poland there was a similar rush of energy to legislate in the heady atmosphere immediately after 1989; the Parliament was so active that it became known as the Factory of Laws. This appetite for legislation continues in Poland.

But a government that is without a secure majority in the legislative assembly, is troubled by division or is approaching the end of a term in office may have different priorities. It may be less likely to undertake complex legislation with cost implications and no short-term rewards, and more likely to tackle immediate issues, especially those without costs attached, which might revive flagging poll ratings.

Not only do the various stimuli to action and the political contexts vary, but so do the tasks attempted in legislation. A piece of law may release the public from various obligations (eg, the deregulation of public transport in the United Kingdom, or the body of work of Andras Sajo, now an eminent Judge in Strasbourg, who was appointed to be the Parliamentary Commissioner for Deregulation in Hungary after transformation, and the emancipatory legislation in Poland in 1990, which removed restrictions on the freedom of assembly). Alternatively, legislation may try to impose new obligations on individuals (as in the example of the Child Support Act 1991, which was discussed above in chapter three). Deregulation may carry unexpected consequences and may be unpopular with some parts of the community. We may see more of it under the Coalition government of 2010. But overall, the setting aside of regulations is often less difficult than trying to impose a new and unpopular burden. The contrast between removing or increasing tax obligations is a clear example of popular and unpopular measures designed to produce votes or to protect the economy.

Furthermore, some tasks may simply not be capable of achievement through the legislative process, for example, the attempts to deal with lustration in the Polish setting, where the issues have proven quite simply irreconcilable. Attempts to legislate to 'cleanse' the communist past and to make a clear-cut division between those who were at fault and those who were not have proved impossible. Political informers could not in practice be differentiated from their sponsors, the political police, whose work included not only political work but also industrial espionage for economic reasons as well as traditional patriotic intelligence activity.

Similarly, the debate over abortion could not be resolved, as there was and still is a clear division between those for whom abortion is not acceptable for religious reasons and those who support women's right to choose. This kind of legislative impasse may be less likely to emerge in practice when a government controls the legislative agenda, as in the Parliament at Westminster. On the other hand, codification of existing laws may be one of the easier forms of law work, as in the Children Act (England and Wales) 1989 (discussed above in chapter two), while attempts at overall regulation of a new phenomenon may be more problematic. (For example, the attempts in Poland to regulate the media after 1989 resulted in a prison sentence for an acclaimed senior member of the artistic establishment.)

4. How is Law Made?

We have shown above in the case studies the different ways in which some recent pieces of legislation progressed towards the statute book in Britain. The Children Act 1989 (discussed in chapter two) went slowly, with great thought and care to maintain consensus, without party political pressure; and it achieved long-lasting codification and international esteem. The Child Support Act 1991 (chapter three) went through the process at high speed, using blunt instruments to demand that unwilling fathers meet newly defined financial obligations, and it was subject to strong pressure from the Prime Minister. The Children and Adoption Act 2006 (chapter four), which deals with contact between separated parents and their children, proceeded in the direction of available evidence, but only through the tactical manoeuvring of officials and despite acute pressure from fathers' groups and some press hostility. The Children, Schools and Families Act 2010 (chapter five) takes tactical legislation one step further, although this attempt to open up the courts to the media may well result in no action at all, even though a new statute is now on the books.

In Poland, the process for achieving a completed statute is far more complex, with rights of veto vested in both the President and the Senate; and all legislation is also subject to review by the Constitutional Court. In England and Wales, even when a statute has completed the legislative process and received Royal Assent, there may be a considerable period of time before any action follows – and there may even be no action at all. For example, the Family Law Act 1996 attempted to reform both the law relating to the grounds for divorce and also the procedures for professional intervention. Neither part of the legislation has resulted in any change.

We have described the formal systems for law-making in both jurisdictions in context, to give examples of how these systems are operated by lawmakers in the social world. Our final question addresses the issue of legislative success or failure.

5. What Works Well, for Whom and Why?

In chapter one we outlined guidelines for law-making that were first set out by Leon Petrażycki and later developed by Adam Podgorecki.[3] In this formulation, law-making should be a purposeful, instrumental, reflexive and rational activity, requiring self-reflection by lawmakers, who use scientific rational methods to monitor continually the possible and actual effects of a piece of law. With this understanding, what can our experiences with the four case studies tell us about what works well for politicians, officials, draftsmen and, above all, the man in the street?

We have suggested above that different constituencies have different criteria for assessing the success of a law. A draftsman seeks to achieve clarity, which can be evidenced by a lack of challenge in the courts. A policy official will be content if the measure stands the test of time and can be implemented without problems. A politician hopes to satisfy his party leader and the electorate so that he will retain his mandate, maintain his position of power and can engage in further law-making in the future. A politician's aims therefore sit quite comfortably with the utilitarian maxim of increasing the welfare of as many of the population as possible, if we accept the proposition that the population can identify how to increase its own welfare. We suspect, however, that the aims of government are sometimes limited to *appearing* to be being useful, by passing laws of mainly symbolic or tactical value.

We have given examples in the case studies of the various forms of legislative success. The able codification of the Children Act 1989 pleased not only lawyers but also policy and political constituencies. Furthermore, the carefully nuanced philosophy underpinning this Act concerning the nature of the relationship between family privacy and state intervention has survived throughout the period studied here and continues to underpin new legislation concerning children.

[3] See K Motyka, 'Leon Petracycki: Challenge to Legal Orthodoxy', 23rd IVR World Congress (Krakow, 1–6 Aug 2007); L Petrażycki, *Law and Morality*, HW Babb (trans) Harvard University (Cambridge, MA, Press , 1995); and A Podgorecki, J Alexander and R Shields (eds), *Social Engineering* (Ottawa, Carleton University Press, 1996). See also above ch 1.

In contrast, the short-term unpopularity of the Child Support Act 1991 was not helped by shortcomings in the procedures adopted and the manner in which they were implemented. But the 'failure' was largely due to the nature of the task at hand – trying to take money from men who do not think that they should part with it – in the absence of any system that could easily accommodate that task. In Australia, the introduction of a similar system was made easier by the structure of the tax system, which provides a figure on which to base a good estimate of the coming year's earnings. The English tax system, however, cannot provide such information, so a great deal of work has to be done to establish the potential payor's circumstances, at a time when these are likely to be in a state of some confusion. Nevertheless, despite the immediate and continuing criticism of the Child Support Act and its institutions for failing to collect monies due and for being slow and cumbersome, we suggest that there may have been longer-term benefits in the greater prominence given to the acceptance of paternal financial responsibility. This legislation offers a rare example of a piece of unpopular legislation, carried through by the force of a Prime Minister's powerful position and personality, which has over the last twenty years brought about or at least reinforced a social benefit – a growing acceptance that fathers have a financial responsibility to their children, whatever their relationship to the mothers.

Our third English example of child contact legislation is a complex tale of extreme pressure on government from certain individuals and that pressure being resisted by lawmakers using research evidence. The Children and Adoption Act 2006 therefore represents a good outcome from the point of view of clarity, enforceability and benefit to those in need of legal protection, but it was an uncomfortable process for a government being subjected to high-profile press criticism. It is a clear example of tactical, symbolic legislation that achieves its objective by appearing to promote change while in fact offering very little.

The final example, the Children and Schools Act 2010, is the clearest example of the potentially overwhelming impact of press interest. Although this legislative initiative had its origins in the criticism raised through Parliamentary scrutiny the Constitutional Affairs Select Committee in 2004, the insistence of the media on better access to the family courts by 2010 had overridden the concerns of professionals and experts working in the field, who made clear their concerns about the need of children for privacy. The law has now reached the statute book, but the prospects for implementation remain uncertain under the new Administration.

Barriers to Achieving Effective Legislation

In the second section of this chapter we move on from the five questions that have guided our discussion of the case studies to develop ideas for further consideration about the relationships between the origins, aims and outcomes of legislative projects. We ask what it is that we want and what we can hope to get from our lawmakers. Can we ask for the Utilitarian aim of maximising benefit to the greatest number of the population? Or should we be content with minimising the possible harm? If the social process of law-making necessitates compromise, is every statute a 'deal'? What are the barriers to achieving effective legislation?

We found some areas where legislative effort has been recurrent or chronic. For example, in the United Kingdom, legislation dealing with the issues of child support has been passed but has also been constantly revisited and revised. Similarly, post-communist Poland has seen repeated but unsuccessful attempts to legislate for lustration and abortion. As time passes we see these issues being raised again and again, with no effective outcome being reached and with continual public debate, which has only resulted in further unproductive legislative proposals. No deals could be made.

Failure to achieve change through legislation may happen for other reasons, namely that the issue is simply beyond the scope of law reform. An area may be so regulated that no further change is needed or can be tolerated for the time being. Local parking regulations are a case in point in English cities. Some issues quite naturally cease to need a legislative response as they become obsolete, such as regulations about steam locomotives, but new issues continually appear and evoke public calls for legal regulation, such as the downloading of material from the internet and the implications for the music and publishing industries.

It is difficult in advance to identify potential issues for legislation as being either feasible or infeasible. The more often and more deeply an issue is discussed, the more likely resolution is to seem impossible, as in our example of the conflict between achieving confidentiality and confidence in the English family courts.[4] On the other hand, a quick symbolic legislative solution may stimulate support from the electorate in the short term, though in the longer term the reform may prove to be of little value, as is the case, for example, with British[5] controls on dangerous dogs.

[4] See above ch 5.

[5] See Dangerous Dogs Act p 9.

Limitations on the Effectiveness of Legislative Change when the Process has been Completed

Legislation may become ineffective when people get used to a situation and ignore regulation (eg, when someone crosses the road without using an appointed pedestrian crossing) or when people develop ways around unwelcome controls (eg, when the highly skilled area of tax management becomes widely developed). But there are also laws that are expected to have symbolic rather than practical impact. We have commented on the increasing use of symbolic law, the *gli leggi manifesti* of Italian law,[6] which is generally criticised. At least one of our case studies fall into this category: the Chiildren and Adoption Act 2006. Symbolic law now appears so frequently in the democratic legislative process that further discussion may be helpful.

The function of symbolic law is firstly to tell the public what is good and what is bad. This kind of argument was used by the British Coalition Government in 2010 to support tax breaks for married as opposed to cohabiting couples. Married couples are then expected to live stable and productive lives, bringing up children as good family members and citizens. In Poland the argument for symbolic law is often made by prolife activists who are certain that prochoice people rarely see abortion as the preferred way to deal with unwanted pregnancy. They argue instead that people should know that abortion is not desirable, and that this message will be sent out clearly and firmly only if it is forbidden by law. The possibility that people might act according to their individual moral convictions independently of what the state tells them to do is not considered.

But it is not just the sanctions attached to a law that are significant, the law itself is significant. Petrażycki's student Jerzy Lande observed that during the Nazi occupation of Poland the regulations imposed by the German authorities that severely limited individual freedom were accepted not only because of the severe sanctions but also because of the impersonal authority that law possesses.[7] From the opposite direction, Podgorecki, in his empirical studies of Polish public opinion, was interested to discover whether people tend to attach moral value to essentially technical administrative regulation.[8] He found that there is always a part

[6] See V Ferrari, *Developing Sociology of Law* (Milan, Giuffre, 1990).

[7] Lande, J, 'Sociology of Petracycki' in Jan Gorecki (ed) *Sociology and Jurisprudence of Peetracycki Urbana III (*1975).

[8] See above n 3.

of the population that takes these administrative rules as seriously as moral ones, even if they are of a purely technical nature.

But perhaps the main value of symbolic law is to those who propose this kind of legislative action. While it is possible or even probable that the issue in question may be short-lived, a legislative victory can be both certain and popular. A political party that successfully goes ahead with legislation, whether granting or abolishing whatever is at issue, becomes the winner, regardless of the merits of the law that is passed. And there is usually a larger ideal that is called upon in campaigning for the cause, which can be used to advantage by legislators, whether that ideal is Liberty, Responsibility, Civil Society or God. The calls for openness and transparency in campaigning for access to UK family courts provide a case in point.[9]

The extent to which legislation can deal with social problems remains limited. But attempts to legislate continue, sometimes not because new laws might be effective in problem-solving but for the other reasons we have described above: to express a view of the world, to gain popularity for a government or to distract the electorate from other, graver issues.

Challenges to Legislative Change

We have suggested that the success of a new statute law might lie in the extent to which it requires clarification, as well as the extent to which it becomes popularly accepted. If, on the other hand, we want to consider legislative failure, we need to look at the extent to which a legislative act leads not just to disputed interpretation but to actual rejection.

To legislate is one of the basic duties of elected representatives; it is not just their prerogative or a key instrument in re-election. In her comments on representative government, Hanna Pitkin suggested that the quality of representation is tested when those being represented rebel against their representatives.[10] When assessing the effectiveness of a new law, identifying objections is easier than defining success. We know if a law has been contested, as we can observe acts of disobedience – whether they consist of individual acts contravening the criminal law or organised public rejection of a law through civil disobedience and even insurrection. Should all these be seen as failure of law? We tend to see crime as

[9] See above ch 5.

[10] HF Pitkin, *The Concept of Representation* (Berkeley, University of California Press, 1967).

an individual act that is separate from any relationship with the legislature, and we assume that the government should control it. But it would be simplistic to treat all cases alike. It may be helpful to look more closely at the social process of disobedience to the law.

Disobedience is certainly not the only form of anti-legal behaviour. Though ignorance of the law is no defence, one would be loath to define an action as against the law if the law in question is not in the public domain. At the opposite end of the spectrum, there are those who proclaim themselves opposed to the authority behind law, whether acting as professional criminals, terrorists or individuals seeking emancipation from a specific law that is thought to be unjust. Law may of itself either incite or pacify rebellion. We might also wish to differentiate between rejection of the substance of a law and a lack of support for the lawmaker.

Adaptation to Legislation and Normative Change over Time

We referred in chapters two and three to the need to take a long-term perspective when examining the success of a piece of legislation. This perspective is necessary when looking at challenges to a law as well. For example, wife-beating, which was an acceptable custom in the past, has become the modern offence of domestic violence, while some crimes of the past, such as adultery, are now rarely a matter for the law at all. In family law, there has been a steady movement away from legal regulation of individual behaviour between adults, leaving only legislation that is required to protect children and other vulnerable family members, including the elderly. There is growing recognition of the inability of law to control the minutiae of social behaviour and an acceptance of individual choice in these matters, particularly in a diverse society with a range of social norms and expectations. Jordi Ribot has elegantly presented the case for the decline of legal enforcement of maintenance rights between adult family members.[11] But matters associated with religious custom and belief seem to be entering the field of legislative activity. Pascale Fournier has shown how the intertwining of civil and

[11] J Ribot, 'Family Law and Intergenerational Family Solidarity: Should There Be Enforceable Maintenance Rights vis-à-vis Adult Relatives?' in B Vershragen (ed), *Family Finances* (Vienna, Jan Sramek Veerlag, 2009) 33–49.

religious marriage codes can lead to unintended outcomes,[12] and the French have recently voted to control the wearing of the veil by Moslem women in public.

Looking beyond family law, financial probity seems set to become the subject of new regulation in the United Kingdom and elsewhere, following the recent financial failures of confidence. The very definition of corruption is currently in the process of change. While it can be limited to bribery, which must of course be taken seriously, some would also include conflicts of interest, abuse of public trust and other types of conduct by those in public office as examples of corruption. There is evidence throughout history of bribery, especially of judges and other officials, but normative and legal changes take place over time. In the days of Chaucer, it was possible to purchase a pardon for one's sins. This is no longer so in the religious sphere, but there are secular options. Jacek Kurczewski once had an encounter with a police officer in a former Soviet Caucasus republic who explained the price that is openly required in order to join the force, after which bribes can be collected from passersby on the road. A proportion of this money then goes to the commanding officer, and some to the police officer's family.[13] Towards the end of the twentieth century, businesses became subject to anticorruption measures, not necessarily because of any specific involvement in public forms of corruption, but because the state began to scrutininse the corruption of employees in one company by those of another. Does this mean that a concept like bribery or corruption should be abandoned because it is changing? Or should we accept the dynamic character of the concept, as well as the need that then arises for legislative change?

The factors associated with the relative success or failure of a legislative process may in the end not be as distinct as we might have expected. We have already looked at the positive aspects of recurrent legislative issues. Now we might ask: can the political need to deal with a scandal play a positive as well as a negative role? The revelation that British MPs had taken cash in return for asking questions in the House of Commons led to expressions of moral outrage and was followed by changes in institutional practice. The fact that the MPs had also pushed to the limits the rules governing their expenses was a personal rather than a political misdemeanour, but the two kinds of event produced similar levels of public outrage. What is important in both cases is the change in the perspective assumed in the public debate.

[12] P Fournier, *Muslim Marriage in Western Courts* (Farnham,Surrey, Ashgate, 2010).
[13] Kurczewski, personal communication.

A successful scandal might be defined as one that changes the public perception of a person, a group or a situation so that behaviour towards them changes also. Similarly, a successful law might be one that changes the perception of persons, groups or situations so that behaviour toward them also changes. The word 'public' is important, because it is not what is felt by an individual privately but that which is shared openly with others that produces the impact. Both rejection and acceptance of the law are public practices.

Law-making is always a process with its own internal dynamics. The original mechanistic assumption of the Benthamite scientific rational lawmakers was that they had not only a design, calculated to suit the interests of the members of society, but also a normative framework within which to work. In other words, if the reality of the law fits the design, the law will be a success. As we have tried to show, this model is unrealistic. The design cannot exactly fit the normative tools, and both goals and instruments change with time. To respect the social nature of the process in a diverse society, one needs to move from a mechanistic to a dynamic model. An imaginary, ideal lawmaker would live forever and permanently change his or her goals, tools and assessments. Actual lawmakers have only partial knowledge of their own and other people's wishes, and they can act only within a short time span. Their 'successes' as well as 'failures' are partial, as is their knowledge of them.

We have suggested that for lawyers, the primary criteria of success is clarity in legislation, evidenced by the lack of any need to go before a court for clarification. For politicians, success is related to the extent to which a piece of legislation will help them to be re-elected. But what about the public? For them, perhaps the fact that a law they demanded has been passed at all counts as success. This point brings us back to the beginning of the law-making process and to the journey from social problem to legislative response.

From Social Problem to Law

Many laws are passed by parliaments on which the public has no view, and only a few are closely scrutinised in the media, as proxy for the public. We need to remain aware of the relative separateness of the law as a system. Though the law is never as autopoetic as Niklas Luhman would have us believe,[14] this aspect of law cannot be denied. There is always ten-

[14] N Luhman, *Systemy spoleczene:zarys ogolnej teorii* (Krakow, Nomos, 2007).

sion between the changing 'system' and existing 'law' that makes people administering a system press for change. In democracy it is assumed that laws are made in response to public demand, but the involvement of politicians in creating as well as responding to such demands calls that assumption into question. Politicians who seek to promote the interests of their party will put forward the ideas that will secure electoral support: 'If you elect us, we will make laws [to do away with something or to bring forward something else].'

Such legislative promises are an important part of a politician's claim to represent the people. But there is in addition permanent interplay between at least three groups of stakeholders: politicians; organised public opinion, such as that represented by the media, religion or local communities; and the public as voters. The media constantly strives to identify news items to attract the attention of the public. The public will become more or less interested in an issue, and after some time the media may move on from a story simply because they have found a more exciting one. But if a more exciting issue does not come along soon enough, a process of mutual reinforcement may begin. The more the public is interested in a story, the more the media will provide coverage, and the more public interest will be generated and sustained.[15] A politician will then take a public stand on the issue, and his or her subsequent public statement will become a story in its own right. Alternatively, an indication may come from a constituent about something that is upsetting the public (eg, the closure of a local hospital or school), and a cry will go up for something to be done.

How Much New Law Do We Need?

No amount of legislative activity can lead to a complete and rational code of law. Law-making in our experience is a continuous process. If law remained static this would mean either that society is unchanging or that law has no impact and is being ignored. If we assume the only permanence to be the process of change itself, then any particular legislative success can be of only limited duration. And if we remember Ribot's warnings,[16] there are dangers in excess regulation in the family sphere.

[15] See, for example, the Batman and Robin incidents in England (above ch 3).
[16] See Ribot (above n 10) and text accompanying n 10 above.

Based on our empirical observations, three factors seem to be of value in considering law-making as a continuing activity:

- Law-making is a collective process, and so planning must take into account not a single aim but the views of various groups, including not only public opinion but lawyers and others who will implement or interpret the law.
- The impact of any piece of legislation is complex and will elicit different reactions from different groups, some of which will be the desired effects and some not; and in some cases there may be no effect at all.
- The process of law-making is an on-going struggle, and it is therefore quite rational to value short-term effects as well as long-term ones. Sometimes a legislative project may be abandoned because it would lead to too much intervention in social life. Any law adds to a body of existing laws, and this body of laws will have a cumulative effect.

The 2010 Coalition Government in London has, for example, announced plans to remove unnecessary legislation from the statute book, as it seeks to reduce the role of government and move towards a Big Society. But when members of the public made suggestions for repeal, many of the laws they wanted to abolish did not exist!

The Polish Parliament continues to behave like a 'factory for laws': several hundred are enacted annually, an alarming speed. And while it may seem a rational way of legitimising the job of parliamentarians, justifying salaries and privileges, there are doubts. European legislation raises similar questions. Are so many laws really necessary? If so, the body of law may gradually divide into particular subgroups dominated by specialists, who will be hard to call to account, despite the assumptions of transparency and democratic control by the citizens of Europe.

To conclude, we ask again the key question: what do we want from our lawmakers as they ply their craft? Maybe we should be seeking from our lawmakers almost a reversal of the Benthamite aim of maximising the benefit to the greatest number of the population. That is, we should be asking them to minimise the possible harm to the greatest number. In other words, as a first principle, we might ask our lawmakers to do no harm.

We accept the value of symbolic law-making, which may be rational or expressive. We accept that law is at least in part a self-generating though not self-contained system. We accept that law may not always be the most appropriate or effective response to a social problem. But if we see law as an element in our discourse, a part of our culture and social consciousness, we think it important, though risky, to observe and comment on the complex and traditionally opaque social process by which it is made.

Law-making needs to lose its mystery and be observed and analysed as a word-based craft with a multiplicity of motivations and outcomes.

The traditional perspective of the modern rational lawmaker still permeates legislative action today, and it has generated a body of reflection that has remained influential. However, when engaged in law-making activity ourselves, we found the rational approach to law-making inadequate for coping with the reality of law-making. Of course, many legal commentators and lawmakers themselves may acknowledge that they are interested not in the reality of law-making but in how it should happen in an ideal world. Nevertheless, assuming that dissatisfaction with the present will continue to lead to a desire for further accountability in politics, including the legislative process, our claim is that consideration of law-making needs to take into account the problems that arise from the social character of the process.

Many of our observations concerning law-making come from a political arena in which the legislative body is the most important player. The Polish case illustrates this well, as it is politically pluralist, and the government is theoretically divorced from the legislature. Most EU countries belong to this category, and a government may be composed of non-parliamentarians. A parliament under this formulation need not include any members of a common political organisation. It could pass a law in opposition to the wishes of a government and reject one that the government supports. In the United States, legislature and government come close to this model. The actual situation in most cases is rather different, but some elements of such a legislative stalemate could occur even in the United Kingdom, with its rather different constitutional arrangements.

In a model situation of parliamentary law-making, however, the rational approach loses ground because even if each individual MP might try to uphold the approach , the outcome of individual rational legislative choices is unlikely to constitute a rational entity as a whole. Voting is, of course, a rational way by which to arrive at decisions, but it may not necessarily be the best way to achieve a law as envisaged by its authors. Parliament is the place where rational political procedures meet rational legislative proposals. But in practice, deals are made. Compromise is a rational form of collective decision-making, but it means that legislators may not achieve their original goal.

Parliaments, however noisy, are not the only places where conflicts in working out the legislative process occur. The silent corridors of power are also battlefields, where various interests and concepts compete. In Westminster and Warsaw, as in other jurisdictions, the scope of MP intervention in the bulk of legislation is slowly being limited. So perhaps we should heed Ulrich Beck, who warns that we live in a risk society.[17] The rational law-making approach with which our discussion began aims to minimise the risk that a law will be inappropriate in a given social setting. But if risks are inevitable, perhaps we should move to accepting the risk that any law when passed will differ from what was intended.

Europe in Bentham's day was full of rulers who enthusiastically followed the Benthamite path of rational law-making, while in England his plan soon disappeared amidst the games being played in the House of Commons. Not surprisingly, his rational ideas were easier to apply in tsarist Russia and in the colonial administration of India. Unity, a centralised power structure, a command structure from above and obedience from below, all seem to favour the accurate preparation and implementation of law.

But in a democratic pluralist society we may need a different starting point. Perhaps when developing a legislative project, we should aim to make the plans and the reasons for them known to as wide an audience as possible. The most important aspect of the law-making process may well be not the law itself but the debate that surrounds it. Such open debate is an end in itself, as it helps people to understand the complexity of public issues. The role of Parliament may be to keep the debate structured and well-informed. We have often seen proposals for legal reform initiated by media uproar, which then turns its eye to other issues. Disciplined debate at the heart of public exchange of views is of great value to civil society. It may not necessarily improve the likelihood of a particular law being improved or passed, and may sometimes even have the opposite effect, but good debate is in the end more important than the fate of a single legislative initiative. After all, if a law-making initiative fails, it can be revived under more favourable circumstances. Despite our efforts to observe, to investigate and to understand the legislative process, perhaps we have to echo Bentham, who asked:

> Are enterprises like these achievable? . . . Truths in general have been called stubborn things: the truths just mentioned are so in their own way. They are not to be forced into detached and general propositions, unencumbered with explanations and exceptions . . . [T]he art of legislation is what the science of anatomy is to the art of medicine . . . with legislative and political reasons each affording to the other correction and support . . . [But] there is no King's Road, no Stadholder's Gate to legislative any more than to mathematic science.[18]

[17] U Beck, *Risk Society: Towards a New Modernity* (London, Sage, 1992).

[18] J Bentham 1789, An Introduction to Principles and Morals of Legislation, http://www.econlib.org/library/Bentham/bothPMLO.html.

Bibliography

Arthur, S, Lewis, J, Fitzgerald, R, Maclean, M and Finch, S, 'Settling Up: Making Financial Arrangements after Separation and Divorce', National Centre for Social Research, 2000).

Barrington Baker, B, Clarke, C, Raikes, S and Eekelaar, J, 'The Matrimonial Jurisdiction of Registrars' (Oxford University Centre for Socio-Legal Studies, 1977).

Barwick, H, Gray, A and Macky, R, 'Characteristics Associated with Early Identification of Complex Family Court Cases' (Wellington, New Zealand Department of Courts, 2003).

Beck, U, *Risk Society: Towards a New Modernity* (London, Sage, 1992).

Bentham, J, *An Introduction to the Principles and Morals of Legislation* 1789 http://www.econlib.org/library/Bentham/bothPMLO.html

Bradshaw, J and Millar, J, 'Lone Parents in the UK', report to the Department of Social Security, 1991.

Brophy, J with Roberts, C, 'Openness and Transparency in Family Courts: What the Experience of Other Countries Tells Us about Reform in England and Wales', Family Policy Briefing Paper 5 (University of Oxford Department of Social Policy and Social Work, 2009).

Committee on One-Parent Families, 'The Finer Report' (Cmnd 5629, 1974)

Cretney, S, *Family Laws in the Twentieth Century* (Oxford, Oxford University Press, 2003).

Department for Constitutional Affairs (DCA), *Confidence and Confidentiality: Improving Transparency and Privacy in Family Courts* (Consultation paper 11/06, Cm 6886, 2006).

——, *Confidence and Confidentiality: Improving Transparency and Privacy in Family Courts* (response to consultation CP(R) 11/06, Cm 7036, 2007).

——, *Disclosure of Information in Family Proceedings Cases involving Children: Response to the Public Consultation* (Cm 6623, 2005).

Department of Health, People Like Us: the Report on the Review of Safeguards for Children Living at Home , Sir William Utting, DH 1997

Dingwall, R, Eekelaar, J and Murray, T, *The Protection of Children: State Intervention and Family Life* (Avebury, Aldershot, 1995).

Dunn, J, 'Contact and Children's Persepctives on Parental relationships' in A Bainham, B Lindley, M Richards, and L Trinder (eds) *Children and their families: Contact, Rights and Welfare* (Oxford, Hart Publishing, 2004).

Dworkin, R, *Law's Empire* (Cambridge, MA, Belknap Press of Harvard University Press, 1986).

Eekelaar, J, 'Families and Children: From Welfarism to Rights' in JC McCrudden and G Chambers (eds), *Individual Rights and the Law in Britain* (Oxford, Oxford University Press, 1994).

Eekelaar, J and Maclean, M, *Maintenance after Divorce* (Oxford, Oxford University Press, 1986).

Ellman, I, 'Why Making Family Law is Hard' (2003) 35(3) *Arizona State Law Journal* 699.

Espenshade, T, *Investing in Children: New Estimates of Parental Expenditure* (Washington DC, Urban Institute Press, 1984).

Family Law Review, 'Every Family Matters: An In-Depth Review of Family Law in Britain' (Centre for Social Justice, 2009).

Fehlberg, B and Maclean, M, 'Child Support Policy in Australia and the UK: Changing Priorities but a Similar Tough Deal for Children' (2009) 23(1) *International Journal of Law, Policy and the Family* 1.

Ferrari, V, *Developing Sociology of Law* (Milan, Giuffre, 1990).

Fournier, P, *Muslim Marriage in Western Courts* (Farnham, Surrey, Ashgate, 2010).

Fuszara, M, 'The Judges Room', mimeo (1980), later published as M Fuszara, *Family, Gender and Body* (Warsaw, 1990).

Garfinkel, I, 'Child Support Trends in the United States' in L Weitzman and M Maclean (eds), *Economic Consequences of Divorce* (Oxford, Oxford University Press, 1992).

Geldof, B, 'The Real Love that Dare Not Speak its Name' in A Bainham, B Lindley, M Richards and E Trinder (eds), *Children and Their Families: Contact, Rights and Welfare* (Oxford, Hart Publishing, 2003).

George, R and Roberts, C, 'The Media and the Family Courts: Key Information and Questions about the Children, Schools and Families Bill', Family Policy Briefing Paper 6 (University of Oxford Department of Social Policy and Social Work, 2009).

Hansard Society, 'Issues in Law-Making 6: Post-Legislative Scrutiny' Briefing paper (May 2005).

Harris, P, 'The Children Act: A Private History' (2006) 36 *Family Law* 1054.

Harris, T and George, R, 'Parental Responsibility and Shared Residence Orders: Parliamentary Intentions and Judicial Interpretations' (2010) 22(2) *Child and Family Law Quarterly* 151.

Henshaw, D, *Recovering Child Support: Routes to Responsibility* (The Henshaw Report) (Department of Work and Pensions, July 2006) Cm 6894.

Home Office, 'Supporting Families: A Consultation Document' (London, HMSO, 1998).

House of Commons Constitutional Affairs Select Committee 'Freedom of Information Act: Progress towards Implementation' " Final Report of Session 2004–5, Vol 1 November 2004.

Hunt, J *Researching Contact* (London, National Council for One Parent Families, 2003).

Hunt, J and McLeod, A, 'Outcomes of Applications to Court for Contact Orders after Parental Separation or Divorce', policy report for the Ministry of Justice, 2008.

Hunt, J and Roberts, C, 'Child Contact with Non-resident Parents', Family Policy Briefing Paper 3 (University of Oxford Department of Social Policy and Social Work, 2004).

——, 'Intervening in Litigated Contact: Ideas from Other Jurisdictions', Family Policy Briefing Paper 4 (University of Oxford Department of Social Policy and Social Work, 2005).

Kurczewski, J, *Living Sociology of Law* (Warsaw, University of Warsaw Press, 2010)

Kurczewski, J and Maclean, M, *Family Law and Family Policy in the New Europe*, Oñati International Series in Law and Society (Aldershot, Ashgate, 1997).

Lande J 'Sociology of Petrazycki' in Jan Gorecki(ed) *Sociology and Jurisprudence of Leon Petrazycki* (Illinois, University of illinois Press, 1976).

London Borough of Greenwich, 'A Child in Mind: Protection of Children in a Responsible Society', report into the circumstances surrounding the death of Kimberly Carlisle (1987).

Lord Mackay, (1989) *New Law Journal* 505–07.

Luhman, N, *Systemy spoleczene:zarys ogolnej teorii* (Krakow, Nomos, 2007).

McIntosh, J and Long, C, 'The Child-Responsive Program, Operating within the Less Adversarial Trial: A Follow-Up Study of Parent and Child Outcomes', report to the Family Court of Australia, 2007.

McIntosh, J, Smyth, B, Kelaher, M, Wells,Y and Long, C, 'Post-separation Parenting Arrangements and Developmental Outcomes for Infants and Children: Collected Reports', report to the Australian Attorney General's Department, May 2010.

Ministry of Justice (MoJ), *Confidence and Confidentiality: Openness in Family Courts – A New Approach* (consultation paper CP 10/07, Cm 7173, 2007).

——, *Family Justice in View* (Response to Consultation Cm7502) 2008

Moriarty, M, 'The Policy-Making Process: How It Is Seen from the Home Office' in N Walker (ed), *Penal Policy-Making*, Cropwood Conference, Institute of Criminology, Cambridge 1977.

Motyka, K, 'Leon Petracycki: Challenge to Legal Orthodoxy', 23rd IVR World Congress (Krakow, 1–6 Aug 2007).

O'Quigley, I, '*Listening to Children's' Voices and Representing Their Best Interests: A Summary of Current Research*' (York, JRF, 1999).

Petrażycki, L, *Law and Morality*, HW Babb (trans) (Cambridge, MA, Harvard University Press,1995).

Pitkin, HF, *The Concept of Representation* (Berkeley, University of California Press, 1967).

Podgorecki, A, in A Podgorecki, J Alexander and R Shields (eds), *Social Engineering* (Ottawa, Carleton University Press, 1996).

Second Report from the Social Services Committee 1983–4, Children in Care, Vol 1 (House of Commons 360–1,1984)

Smith, M, Robertson, J, Dixon, J, O Quigley, M, Whitehead, Z, 'A study of Stepchildren and Step parenting. Thomas Coram Research Unit, London, 2001,

Pryor, J and Rodgers, B, *Children in Changing Families* (Oxford, Blackwell, 2001).

Rhoades, H, 'The "No-Contact Mother": Reconstructions of Motherhood in the Era of the "New Father"' (2002) 16(1) *International Journal of Law, Policy and the Family* 71–94.

Ribot, J, 'Family Law and Intergenerational Family Solidarity: Should There Be Enforceable Maintenance Rights vis-à-vis Adult Relatives?' in B Vershragen (ed), *Family Finances* (Vienna, Jan Sramek Veerlag, 2009) 33–49.

Smart, C, May, V, Wade, A and Furniss, C, *Residence and Contact Disputes in Court: Volume 1*, Department for Constitutional Affairs (DCA) Research Series 6/03, 2003.

——, *Residence and Contact Disputes in Court: Volume 2*, Department for Constitutional Affairs (DCA) Research Series 4/05, 2005.

Smith, M, Robertson, J, Dixon, J, Quigley, M and Whitehead, E, 'A Study of Stepchildren and Step-parenting', Report to the Department of Health (2001).

Snyder, F, 'Thinking about Interests: Legislative Process in the European Community' in J Starr and J Collier (eds), *History and Power in the Study of Law* (Ithaca, Cornell University Press, 1989) 168–201.

Lord Justice Thorpe and Cowton, C (eds), *Delight and Dole: The Children Act 10 Years On* (Bristol, Family Law, 2002).

Trinder, L, Connolly, J, Kellett, J, Notley, C and Swift, L, 'Making Contact Happen or Making Contact Work?', Department for Constitutional Affairs (DCA) Research Series 3/06, 2006.

Trinder, L, Kellett, J, Connolly, J and Notley, C, 'Evaluation of the Family Resolutions Pilot Project', UK Department for Education and Skills Research Report 720, 2006.

Utting, W, 'People Like Us': the Report on the Review of Safeguards for Children Living Away from Home Department of Health/Welsh Office, 1997.

Waterhouse, R, 'Lost in Care: Report of the Tribunal of Enquiry into the Abuse of Children in Care in the Former County Council Areas of Gwynedd and Clwyd since 1974' (The Waterhouse Report) (HC 1999–2000, 201).

Wikeley, N, *Child Support: Law and Policy* (Oxford, Hart Publishing, 2006).

Zander, M, *The Law-Making Process*, 1st edn (London, Weidenfeld and Nicholson, 1980).

INDEX

Index

Index

www.ingramcontent.com/pod-product-compliance
Ingram Content Group UK Ltd.
Pitfield, Milton Keynes, MK11 3LW, UK
UKHW021905150926
475560UK00003B/185

9 781849 462273